The People's Bible

ROLAND CAP EHLKE
General Editor

ARMIN J. PANNING
New Testament Editor

GARY P. BAUMLER
Manuscript Editor

1 Timothy 2 Timothy Titus

ARMIN W. SCHUETZE

NORTHWESTERN PUBLIS
Milwaukee, Wisc

D1082559

The cover and interior illustrations were originally executed by James Tissot (1836-1902). The maps of Paul's journeys were drawn by Dr. John Lawrenz, Saginaw, Michigan.

Scripture taken from the HOLY BIBLE, NEW INTERNATIONAL VERSION. Copyright © 1973, 1978, 1984 International Bible Society. Used by permission of Zondervan Bible Publishers.

Library of Congress Card 90-63674
Northwestern Publishing House
1250 N. 113th St., Milwaukee, WI 53226-3284
© 1991 by Northwestern Publishing House
Published 1991
Printed in the United States of America
ISBN 0-8100-0372-4

CONTENTS

ILLUSTRATIONS

EDITOR'S PREFACE

The People's Bible is just what the name implies—a Bible for the people. It includes the complete text of the Holy Scriptures in the popular New International Version. The commentary following the Scripture sections contains personal applications as well as historical background and explanations of the text.

The authors of *The People's Bible* are men of scholarship and practical insight, gained from years of experience in the teaching and preaching ministries. They have tried to avoid the technical jargon which limits so many commentary series to professional Bible scholars.

The most important feature of these books is that they are Christ-centered. Speaking of the Old Testament Scriptures, Jesus himself declared, "These are the Scriptures that testify about me" (John 5:39). Each volume of *The People's Bible* directs our attention to Jesus Christ. He is the center of the entire Bible. He is our only Savior.

The commentaries also have maps, illustrations and archaeological information when appropriate. All the books include running heads to direct the reader to the passage he is looking for.

This commentary series was initiated by the Commission on Christian Literature of the Wisconsin Evangelical Lutheran Synod.

It is our prayer that this endeavor may continue as it began. We dedicate these volumes to the glory of God and to the good of his people.

Roland Cap Ehlke

Paul

GENERAL INTRODUCTION TO
THE PASTORAL LETTERS OF PAUL

The two letters of the Apostle Paul written to Timothy and the one to Titus are grouped together under the title "Pastoral Letters." A concerned spiritual father is writing to dearly loved "sons in the faith," to men who were especially close to him, whom he had chosen as co-workers, whom he had trained to carry on the Lord's mission.

In writing to Timothy and Titus, Paul shows his deep concern for the future of the church. They are to provide the congregations with qualified pastors and lay leaders. But who are qualified? Paul lists the qualifications for overseers and deacons. He gives them instructions on worship and tells them how they are to serve the members of their flocks, the young and the elderly, the widows and the older men, the wealthy and the servants. Paul issues repeated warnings against false doctrine and encourages faithfulness in teaching and godliness in conduct. Little wonder that these three letters continue to be called "Pastoral Letters" ever since this title was applied to them more than two centuries ago.

Whoever wants to become a pastor will study these letters as an important part of his training. Whoever serves in the public ministry of the church, as pastor, teacher or lay leader, ought to read the pastoral letters at frequent intervals. At the same time no church members, hearing the title of these letters, should pass them by as irrelevant to them. These letters with their instruction and encouragement speak to the entire church. Let all God's people listen and learn!

Historical Setting

Unlike Paul's other ten letters, these three do not fit historically into the account of his mission activity as recorded in the Book of Acts. At the end of the account in Acts we find Paul remaining as prisoner in Rome for two years. What happened to Paul between this imprisonment and his execution we can only guess from comments made in his letters and from early extra-biblical sources.

That Paul was released after a two year imprisonment appears to be certain. He had not been charged with any crime but was in Rome because he had appealed to Caesar when Festus in Caesarea had failed to release him (Acts 25:25; 26:32). In Rome he even was permitted to live in his own rented house (Acts 28:30). So we find him writing to the Philippians, expressing the hope soon to send Timothy with news, confident that he himself would soon come to them also (Philippians 2:19,23,24). Similarly, in a letter to Philemon at Colossae, Paul asked that he prepare a guest room for him (Philemon 22).

We assume that upon his release Paul followed through with his plans to visit the churches in Macedonia and Asia Minor. He likely traveled by way of Crete, where he would have met and left Titus (Titus 1:5). He may have proceeded to Ephesus to meet Timothy (1 Timothy 1:3), who would have come there from Philippi, where he had been sent from Rome. Did Paul also visit Colossae at this time, where Philemon had a guest room ready for him? Perhaps, but Paul doesn't mention it. When Paul left Ephesus he was going to Macedonia (1 Timothy 1:3), fulfilling his promise to come to Philippi.

It seems likely that the first letter to Timothy and the one to Titus were written from Macedonia, possibly Philippi, in the fall of A.D. 63.

2

Paul expected to spend the next winter in Nicopolis, believed to be the one in Epirus along the Ionian Sea. He asked Titus to do his best to meet him there (Titus 3:12). Was it perhaps from here that he set out for Spain, where he had hoped to carry on mission work (Romans 15:23,24)? Although Scripture offers no direct evidence that he fulfilled his intention, a source as early as A.D. 96 (Letter of Clement of Rome to the Corinthians) attests to a journey of Paul to "the utmost bound of the West," very likely a description of Spain. If Paul did indeed visit Spain, this may have been A.D. 64-65, the same time as the burning of Rome with its subsequent persecutions when Nero sought to blame the Christians for the conflagration. As a result Christianity became a prohibited religion.

Paul's Second Letter to Timothy was his last. He wrote from Rome, again as a prisoner (2 Timothy 1:8,16,17). What caused this imprisonment and where it occurred Paul does not tell us. He mentions having been at Troas (2 Timothy 4:13), Corinth and Miletus (2 Timothy 4:20). If the assumption that Paul went to Spain is correct, then he appears to have visited the East a second time just prior to his final imprisonment.

The conditions of his second imprisonment were different from the first. As Paul wrote his Second Letter to Timothy he was "chained like a criminal" (2 Timothy 2:9) and expected martyrdom, "for I am already being poured out like a drink offering, and the time has come for my departure" (2 Timothy 4:6). Tradition has it that Paul suffered martyrdom in Rome either A.D. 67 or 68. Accordingly, his Second Letter to Timothy was written from Rome possibly around A.D. 67.

Not all biblical scholars agree on this sequence of events. Some believe Paul set out for Spain immediately upon his release and visited in the East only once after his return from

Spain. This seems unlikely since Paul intended to visit Philippi "soon" upon his release (Philippians 2:24). Others have Paul stop at Crete upon his return from Spain rather than during his first return to the East. In that case the letter to Titus may have been written around A.D. 66. Whatever was the true sequence of events in Paul's last years, it appears that the three pastoral letters were written during this time under the approximate circumstances described above.

Authenticity

Scholars who do not accept Scripture as inspired and inerrant have sought to prove these three letters to be spurious and later forgeries. They claim that the vocabulary and language style and even the theological emphasis are not the same as in Paul's other letters. They say that the errors against which Paul writes are of a later date and that these letters assume a church more highly organized than was true during Paul's time. Then, too, they assume that Paul was martyred after his first imprisonment and the Book of Acts has no place for these letters during Paul's life.

Since we recognize Scripture as divinely inspired and fully inerrant, we accept Paul's name at the head of these three letters, as in his other ten, as sufficient evidence that he wrote them. That Paul should use some different words and expressions and write about some subjects not treated in other letters can be expected since he writes under different circumstances. Nothing in the Book of Acts nor anywhere else in Scripture supports the claim that Paul's life and labors ended with his first imprisonment. The opposite is the case, as shown above.

It grieves one to see the divine authenticity of Scripture questioned and its contents expounded with a critical mind that rejects what is clearly stated in the text and keeps on asking: "Yea, has God said?" We hold these letters to be a part of divine revelation, and study them with hearts that seek to learn what God says to us through the inspired author.

1 TIMOTHY
INTRODUCTION

Timothy, which means "venerating God," was an appropriate name for the recipient of this letter. The son of a mixed marriage (a Jewish mother and Greek father), Timothy had not been circumcised (Acts 16:1ff). But from early childhood his grandmother Lois and mother Eunice taught him the Old Testament Scriptures (2 Timothy 1:5). On his second mission journey Paul chose this young man, a disciple with a "sincere faith," to become one of his traveling companions and co-workers. He circumcised Timothy not because this was necessary for salvation, but in Christian liberty "because of the Jews who lived in the area" (Acts 16:3).

Timothy was a good choice. The "brothers" at his native Lystra and neighboring Iconium spoke well of him (Acts 16:2). Though young and inclined to be timid, he could set a good example for others in speech, life, love, faith and purity (I Timothy 4:12). He combined special gifts (2 Timothy 1:6) with dedicated faithfulness (1 Corinthians 4:17). Paul loved him dearly as a son in the faith (2 Timothy 1:2) so that he wanted him above all others to be with him at the time when he faced martyrdom (2 Timothy 4:9,21).

Timothy was a close associate of Paul, serving with him in the work of the gospel "as a son with his father" (Philippians 2:22). He was with Paul during much of the second and third mission journeys. He was among those who accompanied Paul to deliver the collection gathered for the saints at Jerusalem (Acts 20:4,5). For a time Timothy was with Paul while in Rome during his first imprisonment (Philemon 1).

Frequently Paul sent Timothy as his representative on important missions to congregations: to Thessalonica (1 Thessalonians 3:2), to Macedonia (Acts 19:22), to Corinth

(1 Corinthians 4:17). He placed him in charge of the congregation at Ephesus (1 Timothy 1:3).

Nothing certain can be said about Timothy's later life. According to Hebrews 13:23, he may have suffered imprisonment from which he was released. Tradition has Timothy continuing as the first bishop of Ephesus until martyrdom under Nerva in A.D. 97.

Purpose

Why did Paul write this letter to Timothy? We find the answer in the letter itself. At the very beginning Paul writes: "As I urged you when I went into Macedonia, stay there in Ephesus so that you may command certain men not to teach false doctrines any longer" (1 Timothy 1:3). Paul wants to impress on Timothy also in writing what he in person had urged him to do when he left him at Ephesus, especially in regard to opposing those who teach falsely. In line with this, a little later in the first chapter he writes: "Timothy, my son, I give you this instruction in keeping with the prophecies once made about you, so that by following them you may fight the good fight, holding on to faith and a good conscience" (1 Timothy 1:18,19). Later in the letter he writes: "Although I hope to come to you soon, I am writing you these instructions so that, if I am delayed, you will know how people ought to conduct themselves in God's household, which is the church of the living God, the pillar and foundation of the truth" (1 Timothy 3:14,15). Once again toward the end of the letter Paul urges Timothy: "Fight the good fight of the faith. Take hold of the eternal life to which you were called when you made your good confession in the presence of many witnesses" (1 Timothy 6:12).

Thus Paul writes to his young associate that in his labors in the church militant he is to FIGHT THE GOOD FIGHT

OF THE FAITH. Timothy will do this by opposing false doctrines that cause people to suffer shipwreck in their faith. He will do this by instructing people how they are to conduct themselves in God's household, how Christians will live, labor and worship together in the church. The ultimate purpose: "You will save both yourself and your hearers" (1 Timothy 4:16).

"Fight the good fight of the faith." Who will say that every pastor and teacher does not need this call to arms? Who will say that every member does not need to join in the good fight of faith that is incumbent on the embattled church in this world? May the encouragement given to Timothy serve the same purpose in the church today.

Outline of 1 Timothy

Theme: FIGHT THE GOOD FIGHT OF THE FAITH

Opening Greeting: 1:1,2

I. Oppose Those Who Teach Falsely 1:3-20
   A. The False Teachers 1:3-7
   B. The Purpose of the Law 1:8-11
   C. The Riches of God's Mercy 1:12-17
   D. Avoiding Shipwreck 1:18-20

II. Instruct and Guide God's People in Worship, Faith and Life 2:1-4:16
   A. Prayer for All 2:1-7
   B. A Word to the Men 2:8
   C. A Word to the Women 2:9-15
   D. Qualified Overseers 3:1-7
   E. Qualified Deacons 3:8-13
   F. Reason for the Instruction 3:14-16
   G. Demonic Teachings 4:1-5
   H. A Good Minister 4:6-10

OPENING GREETING
1 TIMOTHY 1:1,2

1 **Paul, an apostle of Christ Jesus by the command of God our Savior and of Christ Jesus our hope,**

2To Timothy my true son in the faith:

Grace, mercy and peace from God the Father and Christ Jesus our Lord.

We need not turn to the end of this letter to find out who wrote it. "Paul," the very first word as in all of his letters, identifies the author. Who is this Paul? He is "an apostle of Christ Jesus," one who wrote with the authority of Jesus, the anointed one of God, like the other twelve whom Jesus had chosen and sent out (the meaning of *apostle*) with his gospel.

There was no question about Paul's apostleship. He was serving "by the command of God our Savior and Christ Jesus our hope." At Damascus the Lord had directly called him and said to him: "Go; I will send you far away to the Gentiles" (Acts 22:21). He mentions God as the one who spoke the command and he calls him "our Savior," a name usually applied to Jesus. The Father too is our Savior. He planned our salvation and sent his Son to accomplish it. Christ Jesus, no less God than the Father, is called "our hope," the one in whom our hope for salvation centers. As so often, "hope" here does not refer to something that may or may not be realized in the future. Since Christ is our "hope," there is nothing uncertain about it. He has accomplished salvation as a reality.

"It is finished." We can be as certain of the hope of eternal life as though we already were in heaven. What a glorious apostleship Paul had, serving by command of the God of our salvation!

Timothy did not need to be assured of Paul's apostleship. He never questioned it. Yet not only Timothy but others too would read this letter, members of the Ephesian congregation and Christians down through the centuries, including us. We all are assured that we are reading a letter from an apostle serving under the command of God.

As we noted in the introduction, Timothy received this letter. Paul called him "my true son in the faith," showing the close and loving relationship between Paul and Timothy. Timothy was Paul's true, or legitimate, son or, more literally, child. Paul had fathered Timothy, but not physically. Theirs was closer than any blood relationship. Timothy was his child "in the faith." Paul had shared his faith, his Savior, his hope, his salvation with him. Whoever has brought another person to Christ knows what a close, endearing bond such sharing establishes.

"Grace, mercy and peace," what a triad of blessings is summed up in these words! "Grace" is that undeserved, forgiving love with which the Lord reaches out to the guilty sinner, so "that he gave his one and only Son." "Mercy" is the pity and never failing compassion, "new every morning" (Lamentations 3:22,23), which the Lord shows toward us as he sees the misery, woe and distress that afflict us in a world of sin. "Peace" is the freedom from anxiety and fear that comes to the heart that by faith has experienced grace and compassion in Christ. It is the "peace" the angel proclaimed when Christ the Savior was born. It is the peace that fills the heart through the knowledge that God in Christ has reconciled us to himself (2 Corinthians 5:19). This peace is far dif-

11

ferent from any the world can give. It comes to us as the Lord Jesus, our hope, says: "Do not let your hearts be troubled and do not be afraid" (John 14:27).

Paul prays that these blessings may be Timothy's in rich measure. This is more than a pious wish, for these blessings come "from God the Father and Christ Jesus our Lord."

FIGHT THE GOOD FIGHT OF THE FAITH

The church is still the church militant. It must continue to battle against Satan, wickedness and sin. Christians still live in an evil world with all its temptations. Pastors, teachers, indeed, all Christians need to "fight the good fight of the faith." Paul first directs Timothy's efforts against the false teachers.

OPPOSE THOSE WHO TEACH FALSELY
1 TIMOTHY 1:3-20

The False Teachers

3As I urged you when I went into Macedonia, stay there in Ephesus so that you may command certain men not to teach false doctrines any longer 4nor to devote themselves to myths and endless genealogies. These promote controversies rather than God's work—which is by faith. 5The goal of this command is love, which comes from a pure heart and a good conscience and a sincere faith. 6Some have wandered away from these and turned to meaningless talk. 7They want to be teachers of the law, but they do not know what they are talking about or what they so confidently affirm.

When Paul went on to Macedonia, he considered it important for Timothy, his treasured companion on his journeys, to remain in Ephesus. What he had said to Timothy in urging him to stay he now puts also into writing.

Conditions in Ephesus, where Paul had spent more than two years on his third mission journey, required the presence and leadership of his trusted son in the faith. The false teachers in the congregation were causing Paul much concern. "Command certain men not to teach false doctrines any longer." Paul mentions the false teachers immediately and impresses on Timothy that he must oppose them with authority, commanding them to desist. This shows how serious Paul considered the problem. It must not be permitted to continue "any longer."

What were the errors taught by these false teachers? Many commentators propose that these false teachers were influenced by early beginnings of gnosticism (nos-ti-sism) as it was found also among the Jews. This heresy reached its full development in the second century. Gnostics claimed to have a higher knowledge (*gnosis*, Greek for knowledge, therefore the name) which was necessary for salvation. They perverted law and gospel and failed to acknowledge God's revelation as the only source of truth. Whether or not these errors were indeed an early form of Gnostic heresy, let us proceed by considering what Paul finds dangerous in these false teachers and apply this to ourselves.

The false teachers were to stop devoting themselves to "myths and endless genealogies." Paul also calls them "Jewish myths" (Titus 1:14). By speculation the Jews added to what God had revealed in the Old Testament Scriptures, but their findings were pure speculation and so must be called myths. They contributed nothing to knowing the true God and the salvation he had prepared for sinners. The Old Testament contains many genealogies. They serve a useful purpose. Matthew (1:1-16) and Luke (3:23-38) trace Jesus' ancestry to assure us that he is the one God promised to send as Messiah. Paul, however, speaks of "endless genealogies," a study that never comes to a final, useful conclusion. Whoever begins to add his own thoughts and dreams to holy Scripture opens a field of endless, useless speculation.

The false teachers in Ephesus who were devoting themselves to these Jewish "myths and genealogies" were not simply engaging in a personal hobby. They were not seeking to show how useless the Jewish myths were or to refute them. Rather, they must have presented their findings as a higher form of Christianity and with great zeal taught them to others. The result was that their activity could only "promote controversies" in the congregation. They were not carrying out "God's work—which is by faith." God's plan for man's salvation and serving God according to his plan center on faith. The message of salvation in Christ works and strengthens faith. Not so the endless myths and genealogies of the false prophets. They caused controversy and led people away from the simple teaching of Christ that they had heard from Paul and his associates. In chapter six Paul will have more to say about those who teach false doctrines

We must ever be on guard against such who claim added revelation. *The Book of Mormon* and Mary Baker Eddy's *Science and Health with Key to the Scriptures* are examples of such mythical additions that we must avoid. Mohammed with his *Koran* is presented as a more recent and authoritative prophet than Jesus. The Eastern religions propose through mystic meditation to bring you closer to God. In fact, all false doctrine adds to or changes God's revelation and as such is "myth."

Even more dangerous for Christians today are those who are devoted to proving that much of what Scripture says is "myth." If anything does not make sense to their reason or to modern science, it cannot have happened as a historical event. The account of Creation and the Fall, the miracles of

Christ, his bodily resurrection, for example, are said to be mythical. They didn't really happen as Scripture says. Whoever rejects as a myth whatever in Scripture goes beyond his reason destroys the very gospel itself. "For the message of the cross is foolishness to those who are perishing" (1 Corinthians 1:18).

Beware of modern day myth mongers! They may have impressive titles and degrees. They may even hold high offices in the church. They teach false doctrines and destroy faith. They promote controversy and create divisions. They have no place in the church of God.

Paul says that "the goal of this command is love." Teaching error promotes controversy. Teaching "sound doctrine," of which Paul speaks a little later, generates love, love to God and love toward one's neighbor.

The kind of love Paul is speaking about proceeds out of "a pure heart, a good conscience and a sincere faith." The false teachers with their "myths" cannot produce these. Only the gospel with its message of full and free forgiveness cleanses hearts, calms consciences, leads to a faith that is without hypocrisy.

"Some," that is, the false teachers, "have wandered away from these and turned to meaningless talk." Although they thought they had a greater wisdom, they had turned away from that which produces love (pure heart, good conscience, sincere faith). They had turned away from the gospel. Instead they pursued their own speculations which were nothing but "meaningless talk," words that said nothing of abiding value. What a miserable exchange!

Not only was their talk meaningless, but they displayed a confident ignorance. "They want to be teachers of the law, but they do not know what they are talking about or what they so confidently affirm." Here Paul identifies the error of the false teachers more closely. It concerned the Old Testament law. They did not understand its true purpose and use. They confused it with the gospel. It seriously damages the church when its teachers don't know what they are talking about, yet speak with a confidence and firmness that belies that their message is meaningless and false. Little wonder Paul urges Timothy to command them to stop.

The Purpose of the Law

8We know that the law is good if one uses it properly. 9We also know that law is made not for the righteous but for lawbreakers and rebels, the ungodly and sinful, the unholy and irreligious; for those who kill their fathers or mothers, for murderers, 10for adulterers and perverts, for slave traders and liars and perjurers—and for whatever else is contrary to the sound doctrine 11that conforms to the glorious gospel of the blessed God, which he entrusted to me.

"The law is good." What the false teachers were doing with the law did not change its inherent goodness. Paul wrote to the Romans. "The law is holy, and the commandment is holy, righteous and good" (Romans 7:12). God gave it. How should it be anything less?

But one must use it "properly," that is, "lawfully" according to the Greek. Lawful use of the law takes into account how God wants it to be used. We are not to change its content or purpose. Thus Paul proceeds to speak of the proper use of the law.

"We also know that law is made not for the righteous but for lawbreakers and rebels. . . ." This states a general principle that is true of all law. Even governments make their laws not for "righteous" people, but for the wicked. Since the Fall this world is populated by descendants of fallen Adam, who have inherited his sinful nature. Law with its commands and threats is needed to coerce them into at least a tolerable degree of social order and civic obedience. One purpose of the law is to serve as a restraining curb. When wickedness becomes unbearable laws are passed to curb it.

Thus also God's law. It was not made for "the righteous." If there had been no Fall there would have been no need for the law on Mt. Sinai. "It was added because of transgressions" (Galatians 3:19). The purpose of the law is not to replace or add to the gracious gospel promise. As a curb against wickedness it does not lead to salvation.

The law, however, has also a more important purpose. Paul writes: "I would not have known what sin was except through the law. For I would not have known what coveting really was if the law had not said, 'Do not covet'" (Romans 7:7). "Through the law we become conscious of sin" (Romans 3:20). The law was made for the wicked to expose their wickedness. By looking into the mirror of the law we get a reflection of the evil thoughts and sinful actions that have corrupted our hearts and lives. It reveals our true nature.

What does this have to do with the Christian?

We return to Paul's words that the law was not made for the righteous. Are there any righteous? It would seem not. No one is excluded when Paul writes to the Romans that "all have sinned and fall short of the glory of God." Thank God that is not the end of it. He is able to continue, "and are justified freely by his grace through the redemption that came by Christ Jesus" (Romans 3:23,24). "For we maintain that a man is justified by faith apart from observing the law" (Romans 3:28). "God made him who had no sin to be sin for us, so that in him we might become the righteousness of God" (2 Corinthians 5:21). Entirely apart from the law we have been declared righteous and just, for through faith in the Lord Jesus the holy life of Christ has been credited to us. In Christ we have kept the law perfectly, and the atoning death of Christ has been accepted as the price of complete forgiveness. Paul addresses believers as "saints." As Christians we are holy people.

If it is true that we as believers are reckoned as righteous before God, and God says it is true, then the law was not made for us. We are no longer under the law, the law has nothing to say to us. Jesus said to those who believed in him: "If you hold to my teaching, you are really my disciples. Then you will know the truth, and the truth will set you free" (John 8:31,32). Again: "If the Son sets you free, you will be free indeed" (John 8:36). "No law is laid upon the just, and that in absolutely no manner, neither as doctrine, as to *what* he should do, nor as demand, *that* he should do it, nor as punishment *for that* which he might have broken. Absolutely: *There is no such thing as law for the just*" (Pieper, *Wisconsin Lutheran Quarterly,* 1960, p. 256). This is true of the Christian as a justified believer. The law was not made for him.

Can the church then forget about preaching the law? It cannot. Paul says that the law was made "for lawbreakers and rebels, the ungodly and sinful, the unholy and irreligious; for those who kill their fathers or mothers, for murderers, for adulterers and perverts, for slave traders and liars and perjurers—and for whatever else is contrary to the sound doctrine." Who are these lawbreakers? Notice how Paul first lists those who sin against the first table of God's revealed law and then also transgressors of the second table. Paul seems to speak only of gross sins. Is the law addressed only to convicted criminals who are behind bars?

The psalmist gives the answer: "All have turned aside, they have together become corrupt; there is no one who does good, not even one" (Psalm 14:3). "Rebels" and "irreligious" include all who do not "fear, love and trust in God above all things." Many would never profess to atheism who yet are "ungodly" in practice. Although they want to be known as people who worship God, they yet, in their daily lives, place their trust for security and their hope for the future only in what humanity with its limited wisdom and skill can provide. Proceeding to the second table of the law, we note that not only "those who kill their fathers or mothers" but also those who do not honor their parents fall under the judgment of the fourth commandment. "Anyone who hates his brother is a murderer" (1 John 3:15). Paul's reference to gross sins includes every lesser, more subtle form of sin.

Of special interest may be Paul's mention of "perverts" in connection with the sixth commandment. The Greek word means "one who lies down with a male as with a female." Whoever says that God in his holy scriptures does not condemn homosexuality, and some do even in so-called Christian churches, is guilty of perverting God's holy word.

Does the psalmist's "all" include Christians? Had not Paul said that the law does not have anything to say to the "righteous," and we recognized Christians to be the righteous? Yes, but Christians still have an "old Adam." They need to confess that they "daily sin much and surely deserve nothing but punishment." It is the law that continues to reveal the presence of the old Adam and the sins that still plague Christians as they go about their daily lives.

As we apply what Paul says about the proper use of the law to the Christian, there seems to be a contradiction. The law was not made for the Christian because he is "righteous," a new man in Christ. The law applies to the Christian because he still is "flesh," because he still has an old man. Paul recognizes this contradiction in himself. "I do not understand what I do. For what I want to do I do not do, but what I hate I do. . . . I know that nothing good lives in me, that is, in my sinful nature. For I have the desire to do what is good, but I cannot carry it out. . . . For in my inner being I delight in God's law; but I see another law at work in the members of my body, waging war against the law of my mind and making me a prisoner of the law of sin at work within my members" (Romans 7:15,18,22,23).

Thus the Christian is both saint and sinner. As saint he has been justified apart from the law, by grace, through faith in the Lord Jesus. He is free from the law with its threats and condemnation, but he delights in God's law and wants to live according to it. Yet, because he is still a sinner, he needs the law so he won't forget how God wants him to live. He needs the law also as a constant reminder of his sin so that he keeps on turning to the Lord in repentance and faith. Paul resolves the seeming contradiction that he sees in himself and which led him to cry out: "What a wretched man I am! Who will rescue me from this body of death?" The answer: "Thanks be to God—through Jesus Christ our Lord!" (Romans 7:24,25).

Citing 1 Timothy 1:9, that "law is not made for the righteous," the Formula of Concord speaks of the proper use of the law as it relates to the Christian.

> The meaning of St. Paul is that the Law cannot burden with its curse those who have been reconciled to God through Christ; nor must it vex the regenerate with its coercion, because they have pleasure in God's Law after the inner man. And, indeed, if the believing and elect children of God were completely renewed in this life by the indwelling Spirit, so that in their nature and all its powers they were entirely free from sin, they would need no law.

However, believers are not renewed in this life perfectly or completely; for although their sin is covered by the perfect obedience of Christ, so that it is not imputed to believers for condemnation, and also the mortification of the old Adam and the renewal in the spirit of their mind is begun through the Holy Ghost, nevertheless the old Adam clings to them still in their nature and all its internal and external powers. Of this the apostle has written Rom. 7:18ff. . . .Therefore, because of these lusts of the flesh, the truly believing, elect, and regenerate children of God need in this life not only the daily instruction and admonition, warning, and threatening of the Law, but also frequently punishments. . . . Therefore, as often as believers stumble, they are reproved by the Holy Spirit from the Law, and by the same Spirit are raised up and comforted again with the preaching of the Holy Gospel (*Triglotta,* pp. 965-967).

In speaking about those for whom the law was given, the apostle concludes with the general statement: "and for whatever else is contrary to the sound doctrine." The expression "sound doctrine" is used by Paul only in the pastoral epistles but it is a concern of Paul in all of them. Doctrine is sound or, according to the Greek, "healthy" when it "conforms to the glorious gospel of the blessed God, which he entrusted to me," as Paul puts it. The second commandment, which forbids misusing "the name of the LORD your God," makes any perversion of God's word a sin. Any perversion, also of the law and its proper use, perverts the gospel, the glorious message in which God reaches out to the sinner with his blessing and salvation. This message had been entrusted to Paul as a chosen apostle of the Lord. He knew what he was talking about.

The false teachers in Ephesus, on the other hand, did not know what they were talking about. They confused the purpose of the law and the gospel. They were using the law "unlawfully," as a means of gaining salvation. They had to be stopped because with their unsound doctrine they destroyed the gospel of free salvation alone through faith in Christ.

"False doctrines"—"sound doctrine"—these must be the urgent concern of every pastor and teacher. Doctrinal deterioration most often begins in seminaries and parsonages. All God's people need to join Paul and Timothy in commanding their called servants to avoid what is false and hold to what is sound. The salvation of immortal souls is at stake.

The Riches of God's Mercy

¹²I thank Christ Jesus our Lord, who has given me strength, that he considered me faithful, appointing me to his service. ¹³Even though I was once a blasphemer and a persecutor and a violent man, I was shown mercy because I acted in ignorance and unbelief. ¹⁴The grace of our Lord was poured out on me abundantly, along with the faith and love that are in Christ Jesus.

As Paul remembers the "glorious gospel" entrusted to him, he must express the ongoing thanksgiving that lives in his heart. "I thank Christ Jesus our Lord." He is expressing thankfulness to the one through whom the riches of God's mercy revealed itself in a visible, compelling manner. The Lord Jesus had given Paul all the strength and ability that became so evident in his ministry. With Paul, every Christian, whether pastor, teacher or lay person, will acknowledge the Lord Jesus and say: "I can do everything through him who gives me strength" (Philippians 4:13). Our competence for the ministry comes from him who is the true God (2 Corinthians 3:4-6).

What causes Paul's thankfulness toward Christ Jesus is "that he considered me faithful, appointing me to his service." By entrusting him with the gospel, God had considered Paul as someone who would faithfully carry out such a trust. Yet that was not Paul's doing. He recognized himself as "one who by the Lord's mercy is trustworthy" (1 Corinthians 7:25). In the next verse Paul will say why this amazes him.

First, he again speaks of this entrusting on the part of God that involved "appointing me to his service." Service, ministry in Christ's church, comes by appointment, that is through a call that the Lord himself extends. On the way to Damascus the Lord said to Saul, the persecutor, "I have appeared to you to appoint you as a servant and as a witness of what you have seen of me and what I will show you" (Acts 26:16). Today also, whoever serves in the public ministry has been given a trust from the Lord, called by him through the church into his service. Let God's servants not fail to be amazed at this trust and to be inspired to thanks and faithfulness

"Even though I was once a blasphemer and a persecutor and a violent man"—no wonder Paul continued to be totally amazed at having been chosen by the Lord for his service. Paul had spoken evil of the Lord Jesus, slandered and railed against him. In persecuting Christians Paul had persecuted Christ. "Why do you persecute me?" the Lord had asked. We shall let Paul himself describe that time of infamy in his life: "I too was convinced that I ought to do all that was possible to oppose the name of Jesus of Nazareth. And that is just what I did in Jerusalem. On the authority of the chief priests I put many of the saints in prison, and when they were put to death, I cast my vote against them. Many a time I went from one synagogue to another to have them punished, and I tried to force them to blaspheme. In my obsession against them, I even went to foreign cities to persecute them" (Acts 26:9-11). Paul had conducted all-out war against Christianity, against Christ. Paul was a man of conviction and zeal also when he acted as a blasphemer.

"I was shown mercy because I acted in ignorance and unbelief." Paul had not acted against better knowledge. He was convinced of what he was doing. He had followed his conscience, misguided though it was through ignorance and unbelief. That did not excuse what he had done. That did not make his actions any less wicked nor his words any less blasphemous, but the Lord showed mercy on him in his ignorance and gave him enlightenment. The Lord broke through his unbelief and worked faith in his heart.

Paul cannot help marveling at the full measure of God's grace: "The grace of our Lord was poured out on me abundantly." Paul's needs were great but God's grace, the undeserved love that moved him to reach out to Paul, was even greater, more than enough. The well of God's grace does not run dry. A whole world of sinners does not exhaust it. God "wants all men to be saved and to come to a knowledge of the truth" (1 Timothy 2:4). What a shame if we on our part place a limit on that boundless grace by our lack of mission zeal!

God's grace came "along with the faith and love that are in Christ Jesus." Faith and love accompany God's grace. By grace Paul was brought to faith in the Lord Jesus, and that resulted in love for God and for his neighbor. Even before his Damascus experience, Paul had a kind of "faith in God" and thought he was acting out of love for God. Often people are deceived by what they think is faith and love. They consider some kind of general belief in God, even apart from Christ, as faith. The love that motivates them is not a love for God but the desire to feel good about themselves.

By God's grace Paul was brought to the true faith that centers in Christ. Such a faith bears the fruit of love, a love that is inspired by the love of God in Christ and wants to follow in the footsteps of its loving Savior.

15Here is a trustworthy saying that deserves full acceptance: Christ Jesus came into the world to save sinners—of whom I am the worst. 16But for that very reason I was shown mercy so that in me, the worst of sinners, Christ Jesus might display his unlimited patience as an example for those who would believe on him and receive eternal life. 17Now to the King eternal, immortal, invisible, the only God, be honor and glory for ever and ever. Amen.

Paul is about to give a brief but penetrating summary of the "glorious gospel" that was entrusted to him. He introduces it with an expression he uses four more times in the pastoral letters to draw attention to an important statement. "Trustworthy" in the Greek is the first word in the sentence and so receives special emphasis. "Trustworthy is the saying." You can absolutely rely on it, and so it "deserves full acceptance." Paul writes with the kind of conviction only the Holy Spirit works and he looks to the Holy Spirit to work the same acceptance and conviction in his readers. Whoever is called to preach, let him first apply the gospel to his own heart, so that with Spirit-worked conviction he may speak to others.

This is the trustworthy saying, "Christ Jesus came into the world to save sinners." Every word is pregnant with meaning. Every word contains a sermon: "Christ"—the eternal Son of God promised as the Messiah, the Anointed one; "Jesus"—true man, the son of Mary, so named "because he

will save his people from their sins" (Matthew 1:21);
"came"—sent by the Father, willingly leaving the glory that
was his from eternity; "into the world"—humbly placing
himself under the law and being tempted as we are (but without sin), obedient even to the humiliating death on the cross;
"to save"—his one great goal and accomplishment "to seek
and to save what was lost" (Luke 19:10); "sinners"—those
who deserved only damnation. "While we were still sinners,
Christ died for us" (Romans 5:8). What a "glorious gospel"
that calls for full acceptance!

As Paul mentions sinners he has to think of himself: "of
whom I am the worst," literally "of whom I am the first." Is
not Paul exaggerating? We think of Barabbas, a notorious
criminal who had committed murder and was guilty of re-
bellion. By contrast Paul had been a Pharisee, who pat-
terned his life most carefully after God's law. Paul, however, never forgot that he had been a blasphemer and a persecutor of Christianity. Barabbas had rebelled against earthly
rule. As a murderer he had destroyed human life on earth.
As a blasphemer, however, Paul had rebelled against the
true God, sought to destroy Jesus' saving name, had sub-
verted faith and the gospel, and robbed sinners of all heavenly treasure. No wonder Paul saw himself as the "first" of
sinners.

God, however, turned what was "worst" in Paul to a useful
purpose. "But for that very reason I was shown mercy so that
in me, the worst of sinners, Christ Jesus might display his unlimited patience as an example for those who would believe
on him and receive eternal life." What happened in the case
of this "worst of sinners" was an example for future believers. It was not an example of God's immediate and merited
judgment upon the sinner, but an example to show God's
boundless mercy, to display his unlimited patience. God,

thereby, does not condone what is worst in us. He does not nullify his judgment upon sin. His mercy and patience aim at faith and eternal life through Christ. "He is patient with you, not wanting anyone to perish, but everyone to come to repentance" (2 Peter 3:9). What an example Paul was of the patient grace and mercy of God! When we contemplate our own sins, what patience God has shown also toward us! And what patience we must show as we tell of Christ to even the worst of sinners.

As Paul contemplated the boundless mercy he experienced in Jesus and the patient love future believers also can expect, he broke out into a doxology: "Now to the King eternal, immortal, invisible, the only God, be honor and glory for ever and ever. Amen." By directing people to works of the law as a means of gaining salvation, the false teachers robbed Jesus Christ of the glory that was his and his alone. Faith that leans alone on Christ, faith that trusts absolutely and completely in him for salvation, faith that says, "Nothing in my hand I bring, simply to thy cross I cling," such a faith honors and glorifies the "King eternal, immortal, invisible, the only God." We look forward to the eternal joy of praising, honoring and glorifying our eternal King, the only God, forever and ever.

Avoiding Shipwreck

18Timothy, my son, I give you this instruction in keeping with the prophecies once made about you, so that by following them you may fight the good fight, 19holding on to faith and a good conscience. Some have rejected these and so have shipwrecked their faith. 20Among them are Hymenaeus and Alexander, whom I have handed over to Satan to be taught not to blaspheme.

Once more Paul addresses Timothy, his son in the faith and his understudy in the public ministry. Again he impresses on him the importance of the "instruction" he is giving him, instruction to combat false teachers, to make sure that only the true gospel of grace in Christ is taught. That "instruction" is "in keeping with the prophecies once made about you." Apparently Paul is referring to the time of Timothy's commissioning or ordination as Paul's associate, further spoken of in chapter 4:14. Those who laid their hands on Timothy may well have spoken words of "prophecy" about this promising young servant, words that expressed the faithful gospel ministry they expected of him under God, words of encouragement from God, similar to those spoken today at the installation of a pastor.

By following those "prophecies," Paul told Timothy, "You may fight the good fight, holding on to faith and a good conscience." Timothy's assignment involved doing battle, fighting a good fight. The world is not friendly to the gospel. Jesus told his disciples he was sending them out "like sheep among wolves" (Matthew 10:16). In Ephesus too there were the false teachers whom Timothy must oppose without compromise. His ministry would be an ongoing battle against Satan and his forces. "For our struggle is not against flesh and blood, but against the rulers, against the authorities, against the powers of this dark world and against the spiritual forces of evil in the heavenly realms" (Ephesians 6:12). Timothy's entire ministry would consist in fighting the good fight of faith.

In doing battle, Timothy must hold on to faith and a good conscience. Without these the battle is lost. He needs to continue to trust and to cling firmly to the full truth of the gospel of God's revelation. From infancy Timothy had been instructed in the Scriptures (2 Timothy 3:15). He had learned well from Paul, his inspired father in the faith. Now Timothy needs to carry on his work with a good conscience. This he will have as he is faithful to the truth that he firmly believes. The voice of conscience must guide us, but it is important in turn that the conscience is "guided" by God's word of truth.

Faith and a good conscience go hand in hand. "Some refused to listen to their conscience and suffered shipwreck in their faith" (*God's Word to the Nations,* hereafter *GWN*). Whoever knows what is right and fails to follow it, whoever knows the truth but fails to proclaim and contend for it, whoever thus refuses to listen to his conscience will suffer shipwreck in his faith. Paul uses an illustration vivid for him. He had suffered shipwreck when he was being taken as a prisoner to Rome (Acts 27:27-44) If I disregard the voice of conscience, my faith is like a rudderless ship that is exposed to every destructive wind and wave and finally shatters as it is cast on the destructive rocks of error and unbelief.

Paul directly names two of those who had suffered shipwreck in their faith. They may have been leaders among the false teachers. Hymenaeus, the first named, is also mentioned in Paul's second letter to Timothy. He had wandered from the truth by teaching that the resurrection had already taken place. His teaching was eating like gangrene in the congregation and destroying the faith of some (2 Timothy 2:17,18). Alexander was a rather common name. An Alexander is referred to in Acts 19:33,34 and another in 2 Timothy 4:14,15. The one mentioned here can hardly be identified with either of them. Both of the men Paul names were dangerous false teachers, so dangerous that Paul himself had already handed them "over to Satan." They had been excommunicated. How or when this had taken place, Paul does not tell us.

Paul states the purpose he had in mind by this action: "to be taught not to blaspheme." To protect the congregation against their errors, Paul earlier has warned that such men "promote controversies." Paul, however, also has the spiritual good of Hymenaeus and Alexander in mind. Excommunication not only removes from the congregation those who are evident as unbelievers, but it also is a final effort to bring them to repentance. The man guilty of immoral conduct in Corinth was to be handed over to Satan "so that the sinful nature may be destroyed and his spirit saved on the day of the Lord" (1 Corinthians 5:5). We must not forget that Christian discipline is an act of love that seeks the spiritual welfare and not the destruction of the one on whom it is practiced. Failure to practice Christian discipline is harmful both to the congregation and to the sinning individual.

"Fight the good fight." The church in this world is called the church militant. It continues to battle against error and sin, against Satan. It will not escape this war until it becomes the church triumphant in heaven. Paul's warnings and encouragement to Timothy speak to the many Timothys who have been called to minister to God's people in the many congregations throughout the world. They too must carry on, "holding on to faith and a good conscience."

Union in Prayer

INSTRUCT AND GUIDE GOD'S PEOPLE
IN WORSHIP, FAITH AND LIFE
1 TIMOTHY 2:1-4:16

To "fight the good fight of the faith" requires more than opposing and excluding false teachers. Timothy's faith-battle, the pastor's, the church's is not only defensive. It is also necessary that people know how they "ought to conduct themselves in God's household, which is the church of the living God" (3:15). In chapters 2 to 4 Paul encourages Timothy as a faithful pastor to instruct and guide the congregation at Ephesus in its worship, faith and life. He gives instructions regarding prayer, including a special word to the men and women of the congregation. He stresses the importance of choosing qualified overseers and deacons. In his concern for the church, however, Timothy must also look to his own personal growth which will become evident and be a blessing to the congregation.

Prayer for All

2 **I urge, then, first of all, that requests, prayers, intercession and thanksgiving be made for everyone—²for kings and all those in authority, that we may live peaceful and quiet lives in all godliness and holiness. ³This is good, and pleases God our Savior, ⁴who wants all men to be saved and to come to a knowledge of the truth. ⁵For there is one God and one mediator between God and men, the man Christ Jesus, ⁶who gave himself as a ransom for all men—the testimony given in its proper time. ⁷And for this purpose I was appointed a herald and an**

apostle—I am telling the truth, I am not lying—and a teacher of the true faith to the Gentiles.

Paul "first of all" urges Timothy and the congregation to be diligent in prayer. Each Christian can apply what Paul says to his or her personal prayers, but here he has especially the worship life of the congregation in view.

"Requests, prayers, intercession and thanksgiving" are to be made. The four words Paul uses for prayer are not mutually exclusive; each has its own special emphasis. The first word "requests," pertains to approaching God with our needs. God indeed knows what those needs are, but by going to God in prayer we acknowledge him as the one who alone will satisfy them.

The word that is translated "prayers" is the most general of the four. Prominent in this word is the element of devotion and reverence as Christians approach their Lord.

"Intercession" includes the thought of the child-like confidence Luther speaks of in addressing God as "our Father." Boldly and confidently we bring our petitions before his throne of grace "as dear children ask their dear father."

"Thanksgiving" requires no explanation. This does, however, remind us always to approach our heavenly Father with thankful hearts that keep in mind that "every good and perfect gift is from above, coming down from the Father of the heavenly lights, who does not change like shifting shadows" (James 1:17).

We ask: "**What** should we pray for?" Paul tells us **whom** we should pray for. How important it is to pray for people and not only for things! "For everyone" includes the sick and suffering in the congregation, the newly born infants and the dying. It reaches far beyond the congregation, to missionaries at home and abroad, to the starving in Ethiopia and India, to fellow Christians throughout the world as well as to the billions still without Christ and without God, and so without hope in the world, friends and enemies alike. "For everyone"—we will never run out of people to pray for.

Praying "for everyone" includes praying for specific individuals or groups. It may surprise us whom Paul names in particular, namely, "kings and all those in authority." Perhaps he does so because we readily forget prayer in behalf of those in authority over us, especially if they are heathen and oppressive rulers. The Emperor of the vast Roman Empire from A.D. 54 to 68 was Nero. During his reign Christians were persecuted, and Paul himself suffered martyrdom. Nevertheless, also heathen rulers are among those of whom Paul writes to the Romans: "The authorities that exist have been established by God" (Romans 13:1). Christians are to remember that the one in authority, whether he is president of an entire nation or a city mayor, "is God's servant to do you good" (13:4). They need our prayers, therefore, especially those who may seek the church's harm.

The blessing we enjoy when rulers carry out their divinely assigned duties is "that we may live peaceful and quiet lives in all godliness and holiness." What a blessing to live in a country whose rulers provide for peace and for law and order that enables Christians, both pastors and people, to go about their duties undisturbed, "to be godly and reverent in every way" (*GWN*)! What a blessing when the church can assemble, worship and proclaim the saving gospel unhindered by odious restrictions, or war and terrorism! A study of history and a look at today's rulers throughout the world show that these blessings cannot be taken for granted. Let the church when assembled for worship heed Paul's encouragement to pray for those in authority. Let Christian people remember their rulers in private prayer and devotion. God's word through Jeremiah to the exiled Israelites in Babylon was this: "Also, seek the peace and prosperity of the city to which I have carried you into exile. Pray to the LORD for it, because if it prospers, you too will prosper" (Jeremiah 29:7).

In praying for "everyone," the church can know that it is doing what "is good and pleases God our Savior." As the Savior-God he "wants all men to be saved and to come to a knowledge of the truth." We have a compelling reason to pray for all people. We know that the Lord does not want "anyone to perish, but everyone to come to repentance" (2 Peter 3:9).

According to God's will, people are saved by coming "to a knowledge of the truth." No one ever came to saving faith through teachings that are contrary to the truth revealed in Holy Scripture. The church must know God's saving gospel in all its truth and proclaim it faithfully into all the world.

In the first three petitions of the Lord's Prayer, our Savior shows us what blessings we as Christians will ask of God for "everyone." "Hallowed be thy name"—Lord, may your word be taught among us and by us in its full truth and purity. "Thy kingdom come"—Lord, grant success to your word of truth so that your kingdom (i.e., rule of grace) may come to us and to the people throughout the world. "Thy will be done on earth as it is in heaven"—Lord, defeat every evil will of the devil so that your gracious will may prevail in the hearts and lives of many.

"For there is one God and one mediator between God and men, the man Christ Jesus." With these words Paul shows why it is so important to come to a knowledge of the truth. There are not numerous gods, each providing truth and salvation. One, only one, is God. Between this God and us human beings there is only one mediator, the man Christ Jesus, who at the same time is also true God. Who but he could serve as mediator?

Because of sin, we need a mediator. Sin has separated all of humanity from the one, the only God there is. What has this mediator done? He "gave himself as a ransom for all men."

A ransom is the payment made to free, or redeem, someone from enslavement. Our enslavement carried with it the penalty of sin which is death. Jesus said that he, the Son of Man, came "to give his life as a ransom for many" (Matthew 20:28). Inherent in a ransom is the idea of purchase, to give in exchange. "To give his life" is to sacrifice it, that is, to die as a substitute. Peter describes this redemption: "For you know that it was not with perishable things such as silver or gold that you were redeemed from the empty way of life handed down to you from your forefathers, but with the precious blood of Christ, a lamb without blemish or defect" (1 Peter 1:18,19).

"The man Christ Jesus" reminds us of the importance of our Redeemer being both God and man. Only he who was true man could substitute for us and die our death. "Since the children have flesh and blood, he too shared in their humanity so that by his death he might destroy him who holds the power of death—that is, the devil—and free those who all their lives were held in slavery by their fear of death" (Hebrews 2:14,15). He had to be more than a mere man, however, for "no man can redeem the life of another or give to God a ransom for him" (Psalm 49:7). The price was the precious blood of Christ, the Son of God, who himself was without sin, "a lamb without blemish or defect." With such a substitute we through faith receive a perfect cleansing from sin. We are declared righteous and sinless before God through him who ransomed us.

We must not fail to see the full significance of the words "for all men." Christ gave himself as ransom not only for a chosen few. The "all" includes every man, woman or child who lives, has lived or ever will live on this earth. The "all" does not indicate just a faceless sea of humanity. It includes every person you know: your spouse and children, your family and friends, whomever you meet, do business with, work with, visit with, enjoy being with. Christ is their Ransom.

That puts urgency and meaning into our prayers "for everyone." We pray that "everyone" may hear about the Savior who gave himself for "all" and may come to faith in him; for "whoever does not believe will be condemned" (Mark 16:16). This is the "testimony given in its proper time," given by God in these New Testament times to be witnessed by those he sends.

Paul was one of those whom God had especially chosen to witness the saving gospel among the Gentiles. "And for this purpose I was appointed a herald and an apostle—I am telling the truth, I am not lying—and a teacher of the true faith to the Gentiles." Paul was very conscious of this special assignment (see Galatians 1:16; 2:7,8; Romans 11:13; 15:16). The book of Acts beginning with chapter 13 records how Paul faithfully carried out this awesome responsibility as the missionary apostle especially to the Gentile world.

We pray that God may use also us to "go into all the world and preach the good news to all creation" (Mark 16:15). But the question is: "How can they preach unless they are sent?" (Romans 10:15). The church that prays "for everyone" will also train and send out Pauls and Timothys according to the Lord's will. Its members will respond: "Here am I, dear Lord, send me."

A Word to the Men

⁸I want men everywhere to lift up holy hands in prayer, without anger or disputing.

Having spoken of Christ, humanity's Mediator, Paul returns to the subject of prayer. "I want men everywhere to lift up holy hands in prayer." When Paul says, "I want," he is speaking as the chosen herald, apostle and teacher of the Gentiles. Paul is ever conscious of being the spokesman of God. He is not expressing merely a personal wish or desire. What he "wants" he has carefully considered and knows to be the will of God.

The word translated "men" in this verse is not the generic word for mankind. It refers to the male members of the church even as in verse nine Paul follows with a word to the women.

The word for "prayer" is in an emphatic position. We might translate: "When it comes to praying, men are to do this in every place." This says something different from Paul's word, "Pray continually," addressed to all the Christians at Thessalonica, personally and individually, men, women and children (1 Thessalonians 5:17). Here Paul appears to be thinking of groups of Christians. Wherever they may be assembled for prayer and worship, all present will join in the prayer. Men, however, are to provide leadership for joint worship by a group of Christians.

The hands extended to God in prayer, or folded, as is our custom, are to be "holy hands." The psalmist asks the question: "Who may ascend the hill of the LORD? Who may stand in his holy place?" The answer is: "He who has clean hands and a pure heart" (Psalm 24:3,4). Clean hands and a pure heart cannot be separated, although one speaks of actions (hands) and the other of an attitude (heart). But who can claim to have clean hands and a pure heart? Only those who come to the Lord in repentance can. They confess their sins and trust in the Lord for cleansing. Then also, they seek with their hands to serve the Lord in holiness and righteousness as a fruit of faith. Penitent, believing Christians can raise holy hands in prayer and will do so "without anger and disputing," with a heart that loves their neighbor and trusts the word of their God.

What Paul says about the proper attitude of the men as they approach God in prayer applies to all Christians whenever and wherever they pray. Only through Christ, the mediator "who gave himself as a ransom for all men," can any Christian "lift up holy hands in prayer." What is true of all Christians should, however, be true all the more of the men as they lead their fellow Christians in prayer.

A Word to the Women

⁹I also want women to dress modestly, with decency and propriety, not with braided hair or gold or pearls or expensive clothes, ¹⁰but with good deeds, appropriate for women who profess to worship God.

Having addressed the men, Paul similarly now addresses the women. Again as herald and apostle he is speaking not only what he "wants" but what God wants.

Paul wants Christian women to know what truly makes them beautiful in the eyes of God and of their fellow Christians. How one dresses may reveal what one thinks, what is important in life, what is in the heart. "To dress modestly, with decency and sobriety" does not call for clothing that is unattractive, drab, uncomely, or an appearance that is slovenly and unkempt. It rather speaks of a sense of what is proper and in good taste. It shows good judgment, recognizing what is decent and proper according to God's standards. Thus it can give evidence of a heart in which Christ dwells by faith.

On the other hand, hair "braided" in a way to attract undue attention, striking golden jewelry and pearls, and expensive clothes that make a show of riches may tell the observer about a woman's vanity and a preoccupation with displaying and making a show of her physical beauty. It may reveal a heart that is centered on self and wealth.

Christian women are to adorn themselves "with good deeds, appropriate for women who profess to worship God." Their beauty is not simply external, but a beauty of the heart that expresses itself in doing works that are pleasing to God.

Peter, addressing Christian wives, similarly describes their true beauty: "Your beauty should not come from outward adornment, such as braided hair and the wearing of gold jewelry and fine clothes. Instead, it should be that of your inner self, the unfading beauty of a gentle and quiet spirit, which is of great worth in God's sight. For this is the way the holy women of the past who put their hope in God used to make themselves beautiful" (1 Peter 3:3-5). Peter referred to the example of Sarah. Paul could have cited examples like Lydia (Acts 16:14,15), Phoebe (Romans 16:1,2), Priscilla (Romans 16:3,4) and many others. Proverbs 31:10-31 gives a comprehensive description of a "wife of noble character." Also today Christian women will seek to appear truly beautiful in a way that far surpasses mere external beauty as they live lives of faith, love and service that reveal their true inner self.

11A woman should learn in quietness and full submission. 12I do not permit a woman to teach or to have authority over a man; she must be silent. 13For Adam was formed first, then Eve. 14And Adam was not the one deceived; it was the woman who was deceived and became a sinner. 15But women will be saved through childbearing—if they continue in faith, love and holiness with propriety.

41

Paul looks at a teaching/learning situation. Since Christians have been instructed to teach "everything I have commanded you" (Matthew 28:20), there will be many such situations in the church and among Christians. "A woman should learn in quietness and full submission." In speaking of submission, Paul is applying a general principle regarding the relation of man and woman to the specific teaching/learning situation. The principle and its divine origin he presents in the verses that follow.

"I do not permit a woman to teach or to have authority over a man; she must be silent." Here Paul states the principle and makes an application. The application is that a woman is not to teach; she must be silent. The principle is that a woman is not "to have authority over man." Paul is not setting up a rule or law that prohibits all teaching by women. The concern is that she not teach when her teaching violates the "authority" principle.

What is the basis or origin of this principle? Paul refers to the time of creation. "For Adam was formed first, then Eve." God showed that he was establishing this male and female relationship by the chronological sequence in which he created Adam and Eve. Genesis, chapter two, records the historical event: "The LORD God formed the man from the dust of the ground. . . . The LORD God said, 'It is not good for the man to be alone. I will make a helper suitable for him.' . . . Then the Lord God made a woman from the rib he had taken out of the man, and he brought her to the man" (2:7,18,22). Thus God created each, man and woman, for a specific role, that of head and helper. This relationship is violated if the woman were to teach and have authority over the man. That is contrary to God's will as revealed in creation. This is the reason for Paul's "I do not permit."

Paul adds another point. He looks back to the next historical event recorded in Genesis, the fall into sin. "And Adam
was not deceived; it was the woman who was deceived and
became a sinner." Our first impression may be that Eve's
weakness in being deceived is the reason she is not permitted
to teach or to have authority over man. But to understand the
point Paul is making we need to examine the historical account in Genesis, chapter three.

The account begins with the serpent (Satan) approaching
Eve and deceiving her. "When the woman saw that the fruit of
the tree was good for food and pleasing to the eye, and also
desirable for gaining wisdom, she took some and ate it." The
account continues: "She also gave some to her husband, who
was with her, and he ate it" (3:6). Adam was not deceived by
Satan's lies and promises. Nevertheless, he failed to provide
leadership but rather followed the lead of Eve and took the
fruit from her and ate. Although Eve initiated the sin, God
held Adam, whom he had created first as the head, responsible for the fall. There was a reversal of the roles God had giv-
en to each. Eve took the lead and Adam followed. So God
tells Adam: "Because you listened to your wife and ate from
the tree about which I commanded you, 'You must not eat of
it,' Cursed is the ground because of you" (3:17). Thus, in
writing to the Romans, Paul identifies Adam as the one man
through whom "sin entered the world . . . and death through
sin" (Romans 5:12). When Eve stepped out of her assigned
role and Adam did not live up to his, the result was disastrous.

Although God held Adam responsible as the head, he also
had a word for Eve, showing what the consequences of her
action were for the woman: "I will greatly increase your
pains in childbearing; with pain you will give birth to children. Your desire will be for your husband, and he will rule
over you" (Genesis 3:16). The blessing God had pronounced

on them when he said, "Be fruitful and increase in number," would now involve pain and suffering. Because they were now sinful, the head and helper relationship would be seen and felt as one in which man was ruling over her. This relationship now was subject to abuse by man as the head and to resentment by the woman as helper.

Nevertheless, the will of God is still that man and woman each acknowledge the order God established in creation, and function according to it. Therefore Paul writes: "I do not permit a woman to teach or to have authority over man." Paul applied this principle for the same reason to the Corinthian congregation assembled for worship (1 Corinthians 14:34).

Having pointed out that the woman "was deceived and became a sinner," Paul concludes this discussion with the words: "But women will be saved through childbearing—if they continue in faith, love and holiness with propriety."

This verse has been called the most difficult in the pastoral letters and has received a number of interpretations. There is no need to consider them all. One that we can rule out, however, is that through bearing children a woman may gain salvation for herself. For women as for men, salvation is received by continuing in "faith, love and holiness with propriety." Faith embraces the Lord Jesus who gave himself as a ransom for all. It produces the fruit of love and holiness with propriety which is evidence of a living faith.

But how does "through childbearing" fit into the picture? Some commentators see in the "childbearing" a reference to the birth of a particular child, the Lord Jesus. This expresses a basic, important truth and would render a valid meaning. We may still ask, however, whether this is the meaning Paul had in mind.

Paul has been speaking about the woman's specific role as given in creation. She had stepped out of that role, had been deceived by Satan and became a sinner. She need not, however, feel deprived or inferior as man's helper. Salvation is hers, living in the role God had assigned to her. Unique and special in that role is bearing children and the mothering that goes with it. Living according to her God-given role will not in any way deprive her of the salvation that we all have alone through faith in the Lord Jesus Christ. A Christian woman will find genuine fulfillment as she conducts herself according to God's plan.

We add a few comments and applications. The world, steeped in humanistic, evolutionistic philosophy, tempts also the Christian woman to question the head and helper relationship that goes back to creation. She is told that it is something demeaning to woman and prejudicial. Increasingly, Christian, including Lutheran, churches are "reinterpreting" what God says so that it agrees with prevailing views about equality and rights.

Paul writes to the Galatians: "You are all sons of God through faith in Christ Jesus" (3:26). To emphasize the "all" he adds: "There is neither Jew nor Greek, slave nor free, male nor female, for you are all one in Christ Jesus" (3:28). Paul reassures men and women that their status and role in this present world in no way affects their being children of God through faith in Christ. Does this, then, do away with role differences in this life? Some make that claim. God's word does not. In the chapter we have studied in this letter to Timothy, Paul expresses the same fact that Christ's redemptive ransom was for all. Nevertheless, he states and applies the head and helper principle to the way Christians live together in the Christian church as it exists in this world. The truth about our redemption and relationship to God does not nullify God's revelation of his will for our life during this time of grace here and now.

In his letter to the Ephesians (5:22-33), Paul applies the same principle to husbands and wives. In calling on the wives to submit to their husbands, Paul compares the husband and wife relationship to that of Christ and the church. Her submission thus is not something demeaning any more than the church's submission to Christ, her Head. Husbands, however, on their part will avoid making it demeaning, by loving and caring for their wives as Christ does the church.

Peter similarly calls on wives to "be submissive to your husbands" (1 Peter 3:1). He holds out the prospect that the husbands may be won for Christ when they see the behavior of their wives, the purity and reverence of their lives (3:2). Surely there is nothing demeaning about a life that thus brings glory to Christ. Men at the same time are admonished by Peter not to take advantage of their wives as "the weaker partner." They should be considerate of their wives and treat them with respect. This rules out every kind of abusive behavior, anything that might cause the wife to feel inferior. Christian husbands will remember that their Christian wives are heirs with them of the gracious gift of life, eternal life through Christ. What an incentive for men and women, husbands and wives, to serve the Lord Jesus according to his will!

Paul's concern in writing to Timothy is that the male and female relationship may find application in the church, as it assembles for worship and work. Since it is based not on a local custom but on God's order established at creation, its validity continues and requires application also today. "Women will not, therefore, seek the pastoral office because they want to uphold the principle of the headship of man. . . . The Christian woman knows that if she were to demand the right to vote and to govern the congregation, she would be exercising authority over the man who is to be her head. . . . The leaders of our congregations will constantly look for new areas to which they can properly direct the zeal and talents of dedicated women" (*Man and Woman in God's World,* NPH, 1985, pp. 19,20).

Qualified Overseers

3 **Here is a trustworthy saying: If anyone sets his heart on being an overseer, he desires a noble task.**

For a second time (cf. 1:15) Paul introduces his message with the words: "Here is a trustworthy saying." What he is about to say concerning the office of overseer is of considerable importance for the life of a Christian congregation. If a church is to FIGHT THE GOOD FIGHT OF THE FAITH it needs good "overseers." To serve the church as "overseer" is indeed a "noble task."

What is an "overseer"? The Greek word Paul uses here has also been translated "bishop," "superintendent," "minister" and "pastor." Such men are to be "shepherds of the church of God" (Acts 20:28). Later Paul uses a different Greek word in speaking of "elders who direct the affairs of the church well," and refers to those especially "whose work is preaching and teaching" (1 Timothy 5:17). Thus the terms "overseer" and "elder" were both used to speak of the same office.

We must not attempt to identify this position with offices in the church today. When a translation uses the word "bishop," this is not to be identified with the bishop in the Roman Catholic, the Episcopal or some Lutheran churches. The term "elder" also is not the same as those who serve on a congregation's board of elders. The closest to the position of "overseer" mentioned by Paul is that of a pastor in our congregations. The "overseer" was a man who was appointed or called by a group of Christians to preach and teach God's message, in their name and for their benefit. We speak of this

Christ Sending out the Seventy Disciples

as the public ministry. Circumstance will determine the exact form it may take.

The term "overseer," a rather exact translation of the Greek, shows that it was a position of leadership. The term "elder" may have shown this to be a position of honor and dignity. In a general way, "elder" compares to our common title "reverend," whereas "shepherd," or "pastor," takes note of concerned and loving service.

Should a Christian aspire to the position of overseer? Paul says that whoever "sets his heart on being an overseer" desires a "noble task." The church needs young people who desire to become pastors and teachers so that they may prepare themselves through special training for this noble task. This need is urgent. Parents, pastors and teachers, friends are among those who can encourage gifted youth to fill the need.

It is the congregation, however, that calls an individual to serve as overseer in its midst. It must do so responsibly. That the person called desires the office is not the only or major or even a necessary requirement. Paul in the next verses lists the qualifications congregations are to seek in those they call as pastors.

2Now the overseer must be above reproach, the husband of but one wife, temperate, self-controlled, respectable, hospitable, able to teach, 3not given to drunkenness, not violent but gentle, not quarrelsome, not a lover of money. 4He must manage his own family well and see that his children obey him with proper respect. 5(If anyone does not know how to manage his own family, how can he take care of God's church?) 6He must not be a recent convert, or he may become conceited and fall under the same judgment as the devil. 7He must also have a good reputation with outsiders, so that he will not fall into disgrace and into the devil's trap.

As we look at these qualifications, we keep in mind their application also to those called into the public ministry today.

"Above reproach"—before God no one is above reproach. If this calls for sinlessness and perfection, who could qualify? Paul has in mind "consistent, mature Christian living which gives no occasion for public reproach" (Kent). Paul seems to refer here to reproach on the part of fellow Christians since he refers to "outsiders" in his final qualification in verse 7. In what sense an overseer is to be "above reproach" is unfolded in subsequent qualifications.

"The husband of but one wife"—in post-apostolic times this was interpreted to mean that a bishop upon the death of his wife was prohibited from marrying a second time. That is hardly Paul's meaning. Whether Paul was thinking of polygamy may be doubtful, since it was prohibited in the Roman Empire and was not a problem. That it would apply, however, in a society where polygamy is practiced can hardly be questioned.

What Paul says is that the overseer should be a "one-woman man." In the heathen society from which the Gentile Christians in Ephesus had come, sexual immorality was as common as it is today. A man might have a concubine besides his wife. In today's terms, we could say that the pastor is not to be a womanizer. In moral matters he must be above reproach. The pastor who becomes guilty of adultery must recognize that he has disqualified himself. When he repents, he will be forgiven, also by his congregation. But the congregation, too, will recognize that he is no longer above reproach.

Numerous individual qualifications follow. A pastor must be "temperate, self-controlled, respectable." The first of these three refers to more than being temperate in the use of wine, which is referred to later. This is a broader term and refers to being calm and collected in spirit. The pastor does not become intoxicated by what is new and different, is not influenced by every wind of doctrinal change that blows across the horizon. He will not be intrigued by change simply for the sake of change. To this Paul adds "self-controlled." This can also be translated as "prudent, thoughtful." This quality involves not acting by impulse but thinking before acting. In addition, the pastor should be "respectable," conducting himself in an orderly manner. "The most correct rendering, according to modern use of language, would be that he should be a *gentleman*. He should not be slovenly in his appearance, or rough and boorish in his manners" (Barnes). A pastor should be a man of good sense, tact and civility.

"Hospitable," literally, "one who shows love to a stranger," also translated "kind to guests" (*GWN*)—he makes people feel at home in his presence. Guests are not left standing at the door but invited in. The pastor's spirit of hospitality will be contagious so that strangers and guests will feel welcome in his congregation's services.

Most of the qualifications Paul mentions should and will be found in the lives of all Christians to a greater or lesser degree. That they are stated here does not set up a unique standard for overseers or pastors. Their position of leadership, however, makes the presence of these qualifications even more important.

The next qualification, "able to teach," is one that has special application to pastors and teachers. It presupposes the ability to learn. We must learn before we can teach, but not everyone who has learned is able to teach. Teaching is the ability to communicate. Since a pastor is to teach "all things that God has commanded," he must know his Bible. So should all Christians, but the pastor must also be skillful in communicating its saving truth to others. In his second letter,

Paul commands Timothy to entrust what he had learned from Paul "to reliable men who will also be qualified to teach others" (2 Timothy 2:2). Whoever cannot "teach others" lacks an essential qualification for the public ministry.

"Not given to drunkenness"—later in the letter Paul advises Timothy to "use a little wine" for health reasons (5:23). Christ himself provided wine for the wedding of Cana. Not moderate use but abuse is prohibited. Skillful teaching calls for a person's full mental powers. Drunkenness impairs them not only for a time but causes permanent destruction to the human brain. Pastors too must remember that drunkards will not "inherit the kingdom of God" (1 Corinthians 6:10). To those who would be overseers in the church, Paul's warning to the Ephesians applies in a special way: "Do not get drunk on wine, which leads to debauchery. Instead, be filled with the Spirit" (Ephesians 5:18).

"Not violent but gentle, not quarrelsome"—a violent person is one whose temper is short. He is all too ready to come to blows, if not with his fist then with his tongue. He likes to throw his weight around. Not so the pastor. He should be "gentle," mild, kind, reasonable, willing to yield when Scripture truth is not compromised. He is not "quarrelsome," not contentious but a peacemaker when factions arise in a congregation. He applies Paul's exhortation: "If it is possible, as far as it depends on you, live at peace with everyone" (Romans 12:18).

"Not a lover of money"—Jesus told his disciples: "You cannot serve both God and Money" (Luke 16:13). In line with what he had learned from Jesus, Peter wrote that shepherds of God's flock are not to be "greedy for money, but eager to serve" (1 Peter 5:2). Paul also calls greed "idolatry" (Colossians 3:5). The pastor's heart should be filled with love for God and for people, not with a love for money and things. Paul will have more to say about this later (6:6-10).

The pastor who has a wife and children can demonstrate his qualifications to be an overseer by the way he manages his own household. "He must manage his own family well and see that his children obey him with proper respect." The key to a well-managed family and obedient children is that he accomplishes this "with proper respect." The NIV translation refers this phrase to the children, that they will obey with proper respect. That is a possible meaning and says something about the manner in which the father manages and gains obedience. Children will obey with respect when there is fair, firm and loving discipline in the home.

The phrase can also be translated "with all dignity" and refer directly to the manner in which the father manages and gains obedience. The pastor-father, as every father, will call for obedience in a manner that is dignified, not by means of simply laying down the law or even becoming abusive in language or action.

The words in parentheses, "(If anyone does not know how to manage his own family, how can he take care of God's church?)" argue from the lesser to the greater. The attitude, ability and spirit the father shows in managing his home and children will be the same he needs as pastor in taking care of the larger family of God's people. By applying them at home, he qualifies for the further responsibility of applying them in the congregation.

Often there does not seem to be time for both the family and congregation. Let no pastor feel that care for the congregation does not allow him time to manage his own family. He must take time for the latter. God expects it of him, even in view of his pastoral office. On the other hand, let no congregation make demands upon its pastor that allow him no time for his family. Let all remember: being a good husband and father, if God has given the pastor a family, is also part of being a good pastor.

A congregation is to avoid choosing as overseer a "recent convert," literally, a "neophyte," a newly planted Christian. Being entrusted with such a responsible position immediately upon conversion could go to his head. "He may become conceited and fall under the same judgment as the devil." When the devil and his host rebelled, God "sent them to hell, putting them into gloomy dungeons to be held for judgment" (2 Peter 2:4). Pride on the part of a pastor can also have disastrous consequences. "Pride goes before destruction, a haughty spirit before a fall" (Proverbs 16:18).

By requiring many years of training at college and seminary, we avoid calling pastors and teachers who are recent converts; but the warning against pride everyone can take to heart.

Paul names a final qualification: "He must also have a good reputation with outsiders." This requirement reminds us of the "above reproach" with which Paul began. While everything up to now had the individual's reputation among his fellow Christians in mind, here Paul refers specifically to "outsiders." A congregation and its pastor live and labor in a community where the majority may not be members of the congregation. The pastor's reputation is important also among them.

Paul explains why: "So that he will not fall into disgrace and into the devil's trap." The pastor who thinks he can accommodate his own life-style to that of the unbelievers in the community, who becomes careless about his drinking habits and moral conduct, or even his personal appearance and manners, will soon lose the respect not only of his congregation but also of "outsiders." He brings disgrace on himself and his congregation, upon his Lord and the saving gospel. It should not become necessary for members to make excuses for the unseemly actions of their pastor. Careless about his conduct, he becomes easy prey for the devil who "prowls around like a roaring lion looking for someone to devour" (1 Peter 5:8).

"Outsiders" too respect the man who lives by Christian principles that they may not even share. They esteem the person whose life corresponds to the civic righteousness their reason tells them is worthy of emulation.

What a list of qualifications! Who can measure up to them? No individual will have them all in equal measure. Not all qualifications may be of equal importance in every situation. Yet a congregation will be concerned that those they call and who serve them in the public ministry be evaluated according to this divine standard. The pastor will use it for self-evaluation. The church cannot ignore God's standard without serious results.

Qualified Deacons

8Deacons, likewise, are to be men worthy of respect, sincere, not indulging in much wine, and not pursuing dishonest gain. 9They must keep hold of the deep truths of the faith with a clear conscience. 10They must first be tested; and then if there is nothing against them, let them serve as deacons.

Besides overseers, or elders, the early Christian congregations chose men to serve as deacons. How did this position differ from that of the overseer? What were a deacon's responsibilities?

The most likely answer we find in Acts, chapter six. The seven men chosen by the Jerusalem congregation to administer the distribution of alms to the widows may well have been the first in that office, even though they were not called deacons then. They were servants or helpers who took care of collecting and dispersing the congregation's finances, looking after the widows and the sick, in general administering the affairs of the congregation. This freed the "twelve" of those responsibilities so that they could devote their full energies to "the ministry of the word of God" (Acts 6:1-4). Since Paul does not mention the need for deacons to be "able to teach," we conclude that they were not assigned a specific teaching role. Yet Stephen, one of the seven chosen in Jerusalem, did also ably witness to his faith. If today's pastor is similar to an overseer in Paul's day, our church councilmen may come closest to the position of deacon.

We can see the importance of this position from the qualifications required of its incumbents. They are to be "worthy of respect," men who properly have gained the confidence of their fellow members. Subsequent qualifications show how respect is gained. The Greek for "sincere" means "not double-tongued." They must not speak out of both sides of their mouths, saying different things to different people. Their drinking habits, too, are a concern, "not indulging in much wine." Whoever is careless about his tongue and is known to drink too much (which loosens the tongue) soon loses the respect of his fellow Christians and people in general.

"Not pursuing dishonest gain"—as one who administers the finances of the congregation, a deacon must be known for his honesty. Trusted disciples of Jesus, too, can succumb to money's temptation. Remember Judas! "As keeper of the money bag" for Jesus and his disciples, "he used to help himself to what was put into it" (John 12:6). He could not resist the temptation for dishonest gain by the despicable betrayal of his Lord for thirty pieces of silver.

Even if deacons were not called to teach, "they must keep hold of the deep truths of the faith with a clear conscience." The church in choosing deacons, or councilmen, must look for men who are knowledgeable Christians, whose faith clings to the truth as a matter of conscience. We recall the "pure heart" and "good conscience" and "sincere faith" Paul spoke about in chapter one (verse 5). In view of this requirement, "they must first be tested; and then if there is nothing against them, let them serve as deacons." Paul says nothing about how they are to be tested. We are not led to think of a formal testing procedure. Even as overseers were not to be recent converts, so deacons were to be chosen because they had already shown themselves to be sound, conscientious believers. At Jerusalem they chose men who were "known to be full of the Spirit and wisdom" (Acts 6:3). Congregations, then, will not choose the members of their council or board to make them better Christians, but they will choose men who already possess the qualifications listed here.

11In the same way, their wives are to be women worthy of respect, not malicious talkers but temperate and trustworthy in everything.

A literal translation of the first words of this verse would read: "Women likewise are to be worthy of respect." Commentators have debated whom Paul has in mind by "women." Some, like the NIV translators, believe he is referring to the deacons' wives. Others believe he is speaking of women who served as deaconesses. In a footnote the NIV gives this as an alternate translation.

If indeed Paul has the deacons' wives in mind, one wonders why he did not say anything about the qualifications of overseers' wives. On the other hand, there were deaconesses in the early Christian congregations. In the church at Cenchrea, Phoebe was such a servant or deaconess who, Paul says, "has been a great help to many people, including me" (Romans

16:1,2). In this context, where Paul is writing about deacons, it seems natural also to say something about deaconesses. We also note the similarity in the required qualifications.

Deaconesses are to be "worthy of respect," the same as deacons. They too are to guard their tongues. If the deacons were not to be "double-tongued," the deaconesses are not to be "malicious talkers." In going from house to house they might be tempted to spread rumors and gossip. Furthermore, they are to be "temperate" or sober, a word that includes also moderation in the use of wine. Finally, any other qualifications that might be mentioned Paul sums up with "trustworthy in everything."

When Paul wrote about overseers, he did not mention women serving as such. The reason is evident. Women would not be able to serve as overseers without having "authority over a man" (1 Timothy 2:12). On the other hand, as deaconesses they could render valuable service to their fellow Christians in keeping with the order of creation as Paul had spoken of it in chapter two. Congregations will recognize and appreciate the many ways in which women can serve with the special gifts God has given them.

[12]A deacon must be the husband of but one wife and must manage his children and his household well. [13]Those who have served well gain an excellent standing and great assurance in their faith in Christ Jesus.

Paul returns to the qualifications of the deacon. He too, like the overseer, must be a "one woman man," a faithful husband. He too must manage his family well, be a good father, even if he is not called to manage the congregation in the same way as the overseer.

Faithful service has its rewards: "an excellent standing and great assurance in their faith in Christ Jesus." These are not rewards of ambition. These are not rewards one sets out to earn. These are rewards God in his grace grants. Those who serve well in the various offices a congregation entrusts to them increasingly receive the honor and respect of their fellow Christians. What is more, they find great joy and assurance in knowing that they are serving their Lord and his people. They find this joy and assurance through faith in Christ Jesus, a faith that will grow through their close contact with his gospel and their use of it. While they serve and help others, they themselves reap a rich harvest of blessings.

In looking at these instructions about the various offices, one commentator (Schlatter) makes a significant observation. Paul, he notes, does not concern himself with questions like these: "How many bishops and how many deacons were there? What was the sphere of responsibility of each? How did they divide their functions? How should they be elected? Were they to serve for life?" There are no apostolic prescriptions about these matters. In Christian liberty a congregation arranges them according to what is best in its circumstances. Paul is not establishing a new ceremonial law for the New Testament church to replace the Old Testament ceremonial law that had come to an end. The requirement is that those who serve be morally and spiritually qualified. They cannot be the kind of people whose faith and life will be destructive of God's will and word.

Reason for the Instruction

14Although I hope to come to you soon, I am writing you these instructions so that, 15if I am delayed, you will know how people ought to conduct themselves in God's household, which is the church of the living God, the pillar and foundation of the truth.

Writing from Macedonia, Paul is hoping to join Timothy

soon in Ephesus (cf. 1:3). Paul, however, reckons with the possibility of delay. For that reason he does not want to rely on a later oral transmission of the instructions contained in this letter. They are so important that he wants them to reach Timothy and the Ephesian congregation without delay.

Paul is deeply concerned about the welfare of the church. Why? It is not just some earthly organization or gathering. He calls it the "church of the living God." The only God who lives and gives life has called the church into existence and claims it as his own. It is "God's household." Its family members are those who through faith have become Christ's brothers and sisters. They are also called "living stones" who "are being built into a spiritual house" (1 Peter 2:5). Paul asks the Corinthian Christians: "Don't you know that you yourselves are God's temple and that God's Spirit lives in you?" (1 Corinthians 3:16). In the Apostles' Creed we call it "the holy Christian church, the communion of saints."

Paul says of the "church of the living God" that it is "the pillar and foundation of the truth." God has entrusted his truth to the church and wants the church to proclaim it. God will preserve that truth in and for his church. In the explanation to the Third Article, Luther gives a simple commentary of this verse about the church: "In the same way, he calls, gathers, enlightens, and sanctifies the whole Christian church on earth, and keeps it with Jesus Christ in the one true faith." Thus God makes the church "the pillar and foundation of the truth." He preserves the truth in its midst, and God's family will be concerned to preserve that truth against destructive error.

But isn't "the church of the living God" invisible? It is composed of believers, and only God knows those who are his by faith. Yet when Paul instructs Timothy as to "how people ought to conduct themselves in God's household" he has the Ephesian congregation in mind. He is not thinking of it simply as an outward gathering of people, however. The Ephesian congregation is indeed the "church of the living God"; for where the truth of God is proclaimed, it will work and preserve faith; the family of God is there. Thus we can apply these words also to our congregations. How important it is for us also to think of our congregations not simply as organizations and corporations that people join. We are a family of God gathered about his word. The "church of the living God" is present and everything Paul writes about how we should conduct ourselves applies.

> [16]Beyond all question, the mystery of godliness is great:
> He appeared in a body,
>   was vindicated by the Spirit,
> was seen by angels,
>   was preached among the nations,
> was believed on in the world,
>   was taken up in glory.

In this verse Paul briefly sums up the truth God has entrusted to his church. He calls it the "mystery of godliness," the mystery of our faith or religion. It is a mystery indeed, which we can know only by revelation of God. God has revealed it in Christ; in fact, Christ Jesus himself is that mystery. Paul, in poetic form, possibly a hymn verse used by the early Christians, describes this "mystery."

The content of the verse shows that it is describing the Son of God who came as the world's Savior, even though he is not directly named. It was the eternal Son of God who "appeared in a body." "The Word became flesh and made his dwelling among us" (John 1:14). When Jesus became "flesh," he humbled himself and lived among us like an ordinary human being. When he claimed to be the Son of God, his enemies accused him of blaspheming, because he, a mere man, was making himself God (John 10:33). They condemned him to death for this "blasphemy" (Mark 14:64).

He who appeared "in flesh" like one of us "was vindicated by the Spirit," literally "was justified in spirit." When God raised Jesus from the dead, Jesus was justified or vindicated. His resurrection proved that he was not a blasphemer but indeed the Son of God as he had claimed. By capitalizing "Spirit," the NIV interprets this to mean that the vindicating was accomplished by the Holy Spirit. This is a possible meaning. Another interpreter, recognizing that "in spirit" seems to be in antithesis to "in flesh" writes: "Christ was manifest in flesh, that is, he appeared in this world as a lowly, despised and weak human being. But he was justified in spirit, that is, he was publicly vindicated by God as Lord and Christ (Acts 2:36) in that new glorified, spiritual state in which he appeared to his disciples after his resurrection" (Becker).

He "was seen by angels." Angels are messengers. These may be God's special messengers the holy angels. The same word in Greek also refers to human beings sent as messengers. Jesus, for example, sent several of his disciples as messengers (angels) to a Samaritan village to get things ready for him (Luke 9:52). Similarly the "angels" of the seven churches to whom John writes in the book of Revelation are the pastors of those churches.

That the risen, glorified Jesus appeared to the holy angels is true. We think, for example, of his resurrection and ascension. Yet it seems more likely that "angels" here refers to the earthly messengers to whom Jesus appeared after his resurrection. Paul takes special note of such appearances in 1 Corinthians 15:5-8. Those messengers were designated as his witnesses and sent out to preach the gospel in all the world.

That leads to the next statement: "was preached among the nations." Jesus was the Savior not only of his chosen nation, the Jews; but the believers were sent into all the world to preach the crucified and risen Christ, with amazing results. He "was believed on in the world." Yes, the preaching of the gospel will be effective until the end of time.

This Lord Jesus "was taken up in glory." He ascended to take his place at the right hand of God "in the heavenly realms, far above all rule and authority, power and dominion . . . to be head over everything for the church" (Ephesians 1:20-22).

He, the Lord Jesus, and all that can be said about him, is "the mystery of godliness." He is what "godliness," our Christian faith and religion, is all about. All of this is "great," indeed, "beyond all question." The church is the pillar and foundation of that glorious truth, the saving truth entrusted to the church to preserve and proclaim.

Demonic Teachings

4 **The Spirit clearly says that in later times some will abandon the faith and follow deceiving spirits and things taught by demons. [2]Such teachings come through hypocritical liars, whose consciences have been seared as with a hot iron. [3]They forbid people to marry and order them to abstain from certain foods, which God created to be received with thanksgiving by those who believe and who know the truth. [4]For everything God created is good, and nothing is to be rejected if it is received with thanksgiving, [5]because it is consecrated by the word of God and prayer.**

In our times the Holy Spirit speaks to us by means of the sacred Scriptures but before all the New Testament Scriptures had been written and assembled he at times spoke directly to his church. How he spoke to the early church we do not know, but that he did so is asserted by Paul and reported repeatedly in the Book of Acts (e.g., 13:2; 20:22; 21:11). The Spirit spoke "clearly," in some explicit manner, so that the people could know with certainty what the Spirit was saying to them.

The Spirit warns against those who will "abandon the faith and follow deceiving spirits and things taught by demons." What a damning exchange: to stop believing the truth as revealed by the Holy Spirit and to follow deceptive lies taught by the devil! Those who spread such errors are "hypocritical liars." They want their lies to appear as God's truth. They even quote Scripture in their attempt to make it appear so. That is hypocrisy. One would expect that their conscience would trouble them, but it has been dulled, deadened, "seared as with a hot iron." No longer is it sensitive to God's revealed truth. With unconscionable skill they twist God's truth to serve their lies.

Paul refers to specific demonic teachings. "They forbid people to marry and order them to abstain from certain foods." They present celibacy and fasting as a higher form of piety. Sexual relations, even in marriage, and serving the body by enjoying food are considered degrading if not evil.

Such teachings would arise "in later times." Gnostics in the next century considered the human physical body and the entire material world as evil. This led to teachings such as those described by Paul. One cannot help thinking also of the ascetic practices in Roman Catholicism, the prohibition of marriage to the priests, its fasting practices, the monastic life. Such teachings are demonic, for they turn the hearts and minds of people to supposed works of piety and away from the perfect redemption effected by Christ.

These teachings are demonic also in failing to give glory to God for his good creation, a judgment God himself made upon its completion (Genesis 1:31) and Paul repeats here: "For everything God created is good." "Those who believe and who know the truth" will rather receive and enjoy God's gifts with thanksgiving.

Believers will not reject any of God's creation as something evil in itself. Sinners that we are, however, the bodies God gave us and the material gifts we receive we only too readily use in an evil and sinful way. God created us as male and female for a good purpose in marriage. Sexual promiscuity, homosexuality, living together outside marriage are abuses of this blessing. Gluttony and drunkenness are misuses of the gift of food and drink. The fault is not in God's creation. Man's sinful abuse is at fault.

Believers will recognize God's creation as good and acknowledge him as the Giver. In prayer they will ask their heavenly Father's word of blessing on the food they eat, on their marriage, on everything the Lord gives for their bodily welfare. Thus what appears so earthly, material, unspiritual is "consecrated by the word of God and prayer." The Christian's entire life becomes a worship of God. Whether he eats or drinks, or whatever he does, at work or during leisure hours, he does all to God's glory. Table prayers, for example, are not just a "nice" tradition. They implore the Lord's blessings and express our thanksgiving. Christians will feel a need for them.

A Good Minister

6If you point these things out to the brothers, you will be a good minister of Christ Jesus, brought up in the truths of the faith and of the good teaching that you have followed. 7Have nothing to do with godless myths and old wives' tales; rather, train yourself to be godly. 8For physical training is of some value, but godliness has value for all things, holding promise for both the present life and the life to come.

9This is a trustworthy saying that deserves full acceptance 10(and for this we labor and strive), that we have put our hope in the living God, who is the Savior of all men, and especially of those who believe.

Paul continues by encouraging Timothy, reminding him that if he points out "these things to the brothers" he will be a "good minister of Christ Jesus." These are words that can serve as encouragement to every pastor, to everyone who serves the Lord Jesus.

What is Timothy to point out to his fellow believers? Paul had been warning against demonic teachings. Earlier he had spoken of the "mystery of godliness," about Jesus and the work he accomplished for our salvation. A pastor will do both, preach the wonderful gospel of forgiveness in Jesus and warn against errors that destroy the gospel and faith. That makes him a "good minister," one who truly serves the Lord Jesus.

If Timothy is to do this well, he himself also needs to be nourished and trained, "brought up in the truths of the faith and the good teaching that you have followed." Timothy is to feed himself spiritually on the truth, the good teaching that is found in God's revelation. From infancy he had known the Holy Scriptures (2 Timothy 3:15). Furthermore, what he had learned and followed, even if it was from the time he was a child, he should keep on studying and reviewing in order to feed his soul and nourish his faith.

Pastors need to keep on recharging their own batteries. That gives spark and life and vigor to their preaching and ministry. They can only give what they have first received from Christ and his word of life.

Paul again refers to the "myths and endless genealogies" he spoke of earlier (1:4). Here he calls them "godless," or profane and worldly. They are "old wives' tales," have no basis in truth, are fictitious, silly, not worth telling. Timothy should stay away from them. They will not nourish his faith but may draw him away from the truth. The same can be said of much that appears in religious publications today. A pastor will be selective in what he reads and studies during the limited time available to him.

From the illustration of nourishment, Paul now proceeds to the picture of exercising. "Train yourself to be godly." The Greek word for "train" is found in our word "gymnastics." Whoever expects to participate in the Olympics knows this requires difficult and hard physical training and exercise.

"Physical training is of some value," also for the "minister of Christ." The pastor who does not take care of his body may cut short his time of service through such neglect. Yet the value of physical exercise and training is limited.

What is important is training to be godly. "Godliness," and this is not something we do on our own but consists in the faith and life God works in us, "has value for all things." The "all" is comprehensive. It includes both this present life and the life to come. What wonderful promises of God's abiding love and concern the Christian has for his life on earth! What a glorious promise for the eternal life to come! There simply is no comparison between what has "some value" and what has "value for all things." Yet how easily we are distracted from spirituality and godliness to what is of value only for the body and this life!

The surpassing value of godliness is important to remember. "This is a trustworthy saying that deserves full acceptance." It deserves to be believed by every Christian without any doubt. In fact, that is what gives Paul and Timothy, and every pastor, teacher and Christian the will to "labor and strive." As Paul says it, "We have put our hope in the living God, who is the Savior of all men, and especially of those who believe." The living God is the Savior of all men, for the Lord Jesus gave himself as a ransom for all (2:6). Not all, however, enter into salvation. He is the Savior especially of those who believe, not because their faith makes them worthy of it, but because unbelief rejects God's blessing.

Personal Growth

11Command and teach these things. 12Don't let anyone look down on you because you are young, but set an example for the believers in speech, in life, in love, in faith and in purity. 13Until I come, devote yourself to the public reading of Scripture, to preaching and to teaching. 14Do not neglect your gift, which was given you through a prophetic message when the body of elders laid their hands on you.

All the things Paul has been writing Timothy is to "command and teach." He is to instruct the elders, deacons and people in these matters, not with legalistic authoritarianism but with certainty and conviction. This was a heavy responsibility, especially for a man who was still young. Timothy was perhaps in his early thirties, no doubt younger than many whom he was to "command and teach."

"Don't let anyone look down on you because you are young," Paul advised. The young pastor who has just graduated from the seminary will appreciate this encouragement of Paul. He may feel young and inexperienced. Members may even refer to his youth. An elderly lady once rejected the correction of her young pastor by saying, "I'm old enough to be your grandmother."

How was Timothy to prevent such "looking down on him"? "It is not our job to forbid them to despise us. It is our job not to give others an opportunity to despise" (Luther). But how was Timothy to avoid giving such an opportunity? He was to set a personal example and to grow in his spiritual life.

He That Is of God Hears God's Words

"Set an example for the believers in speech"—whether in the pulpit, classroom or private conversation, "in life"—by practicing what he preached, "in love"—the self-sacrificing love characteristic of Christ Jesus, "in faith"—that trusts God and is the source of the Christian's life and love, "in purity"—giving no occasion for even a suspicion of immorality. Through such exemplary behavior, Timothy, the young pastor, will gain the respect of the believers he serves. But who is capable of all this? The "good minister" prays: "Lord, guide me and give me strength."

Strength comes from the word. Timothy is to occupy himself with it. "Until I come [cf. 3:14], devote yourself to the public reading of Scripture, to preaching and to teaching." One of the blessings of the ministry is that one can occupy oneself with the word of God both in private study and in the various pastoral duties. The latter are not mere professional activities. The sermon the pastor prepares he preaches first to himself. The lesson he prepares to teach others informs and inspires and strengthens also the pastor's faith.

Paul further encourages young Timothy by reminding him of the gift God had given him for his ministry. He spoke of this already in chapter 1:18. He referred to it again in his second letter to Timothy where he wrote: "For this reason I remind you to fan into flame the gift of God, which is in you through the laying on of my hands" (1:6). Had God given Paul a special word of inspiration to speak to Timothy as he laid his hands on him at the time of his ordination, and to the other elders who laid their hands on him? Did they speak a word about a special gift for the ministry God gave Timothy? What exactly was this gift? The details we don't know, but what an encouragement to remember that God had "gifted" him for the work he was doing! Don't neglect to use it, Timothy is told. By using this gift, it is fanned into flame, grows and benefits those served.

Every pastor and teacher, every Christian has been "gifted" by God. Not all have the same gifts. Not all have them to the same degree. But everyone has been given a gift that is useful in the Lord's kingdom. Let no one say, "There is nothing I can do."

¹⁵Be diligent in these matters; give yourself wholly to them, so that everyone may see your progress. ¹⁶Watch your life and doctrine closely. Persevere in them, because if you do, you will save both yourself and your hearers.

As Timothy devotes himself diligently to the study and teaching of the word and to his ministry, he will grow spiritually. Without any special effort on Timothy's part to display this, his growth will become evident to all. People will forget that he is young and recognize and respect him for his increasing spiritual maturity.

How important it is for Timothy to keep careful watch over himself, his life and his teaching! How important to persevere in all these matters! "You will save both yourself and your hearers." He would do so not indeed by his own works, but by looking to and leading people to the Lord Jesus in faith. "Salvation is found in no one else, for there is no other name under heaven given to men by which we must be saved" (Acts 4:12).

Let the young pastor also today find direction and encouragement in these words of Paul to Timothy. This is encouragement to fight the good fight of faith as he carries out his ministry. Let him devote himself with diligence to the inspired word. Let him watch his life and teaching closely so that he is an example for the believers. Let him not neglect the gifts given to him by the Holy Spirit. He will continue to grow and mature spiritually. This will become evident also to his congregation and will be a blessing to him and his hearers, eternally.

BE A PASTOR TO PEOPLE OF ALL KINDS
1 TIMOTHY 5:1-6:19

In his work at Ephesus Timothy will serve not only the church as a whole. He will teach and preach not only to the assembled congregation, or to groups of believers. Timothy will also serve individuals or individual groups. He will exhort, rebuke, admonish, comfort, counsel each fellow Christian at Ephesus according to need. He will serve individuals in whatever station in life they may be, whether male or female, young or old, married or widowed, servant or free, rich or poor. In fighting the good fight of faith Timothy will serve the individual sheep of the flock as a loving, concerned, caring shepherd.

Different Age Groups

5 **Do not rebuke an older man harshly, but exhort him as if he were your father. Treat younger men as brothers, ²older women as mothers, and younger women as sisters, with absolute purity.**

There will be times when Timothy must admonish an older man or woman. In writing to Titus, Paul refers to some specific things about which older men and women may need to be taught and corrected (see Titus 2:2,3). In exhorting and correcting older people, Timothy, as a young man, should show the honor and respect due according to the fourth commandment. "Rise in the presence of the aged, show respect for the elderly" (Leviticus 19:32).

The younger men and women, around the same age as Timothy, he should treat like family, as though they were brothers and sisters. Concerning the latter Paul adds "with all purity." Not that Timothy had shown himself indiscreet over against young women, but let no one consider himself beyond the need for such a warning, particularly to avoid even the appearance of impurity.

What Paul writes to his young associate every young pastor may apply to himself as in his congregation he ministers to people of many ages. If Timothy had been older, Paul might have advised him to treat the elderly as brothers and sisters and younger people as sons and daughters.

Widows

The first special group about whom Paul writes are the widows. In the Jerusalem congregation, too, they were the first group that needed to be served in a special way (Acts 6). If a woman lost her husband, she lost her means of support. There was no social security, no pension, no insurance, no governmental assistance program that would take care of her. In general there was little if any opportunity for her to seek gainful employment. It is not surprising that Paul has special words of instruction regarding widows.

³Give proper recognition to those widows who are really in need. ⁴But if a widow has children or grandchildren, these should learn first of all to put their religion into practice by caring for their own family and so repaying their parents and grandparents, for this is pleasing to God. ⁵The widow who is really in need and left all alone puts her hope in God and continues night and day to pray and to ask God for help. ⁶But the widow who lives for pleasure is dead even while she lives. ⁷Give the people these instructions, too, so that no one may be open to blame. ⁸If anyone does not provide for his relatives, and es-

pecially for his immediate family, he has denied the faith and is worse than an unbeliever.

In these verses Paul groups the widows into two categories. There is "the widow who is really in need and left all alone." Then there is the widow who is not alone but has children and grandchildren, who has a family and relatives to look after her.

The congregation is to "give proper recognition to" the "real widow," who has no children, no family or relatives. Such a "real widow" recognizes her dependence on God. She "puts her hope in God and continues night and day to pray and to ask God for help." We are reminded of Anna, who "never left the temple but worshiped night and day, fasting and praying" (Luke 2:37).

God wishes to answer the "real widow's" prayers through her brothers and sisters in Christ. They are the only family she has. The word that is translated "give proper recognition" literally means "to honor, show respect, venerate." While this calls for spiritual and emotional support, it surely extends also to financial assistance on the part of the congregation. Paul will come back to this in verse 16.

Instead of turning to God a widow may seek to satisfy her emotional, social and perhaps even financial needs by a life of pleasure. Of her Paul says that she "is dead even while she lives." She may think that she is really experiencing life, but sin has killed faith in her heart. Of course, the church's responsibility in such cases is an earnest call to repentance.

The situation is quite different if a widow has children and grandchildren. She is not a "real widow" like the one who is left alone. Paul states what "is pleasing to God" in such situations: "These should learn first of all to put their religion into practice by caring for their own family and so repaying their parents and grandparents." Even unbelievers recognize the closeness of family bonds and the responsibilities incumbent on parents and children toward one another so that anyone who "does not provide for his relatives, and especially for his immediate family . . . has denied the faith and is worse than an unbeliever."

Paul does not go into detail to prescribe exactly what children should do for their parents and parents for their children. This will vary from family to family according to need. It may be quite different in our society from what it was at Paul's time. Many questions arise. To what extent must children provide financially for aging parents? Must they take them into their own homes? Should parents neglect their own children to look after a father or mother? Should children permit parents to receive government assistance? Is it a lack of love to place a parent into a nursing home? To these and similar questions the answers are not simple. They are not always the same. Let the answers, however, accord with the spirit that is evident in Luther's explanation of the Fourth Commandment: "We should fear and love God that we do not dishonor or anger our parents and others in authority, but honor, serve and obey them, and give them love and respect."

9No widow may be put on the list of widows unless she is over sixty, has been faithful to her husband, 10and is well known for her good deeds, such as bringing up children, showing hospitality, washing the feet of the saints, helping those in trouble and devoting herself to all kinds of good deeds.

11As for younger widows, do not put them on such a list. For when their sensual desires overcome their dedication to Christ, they want to marry. 12Thus they bring judgment on themselves, because they have broken their first pledge. 13Besides, they get into the habit of being idle and going about

**from house to house. And not only do they become idlers, but
also gossips and busybodies, saying things they ought not to.
[14]So I counsel younger widows to marry, to have children, to
manage their homes and to give the enemy no opportunity for
slander. [15]Some have in fact already turned away to follow
Satan.**

In these verses Paul again divides widows into two groups,
here according to age. Those over sixty "may be put on the
list of widows," the younger are advised to marry. There
may, of course, be "real widows" or widows with family in
either of these age groups. Paul does not seem to have divided all widows into mutually exclusive groups.

We wish we knew more about what it meant to put a widow on the list. What kind of list was this? Commentators
generally follow one of two explanations. Some consider this
a list of those widows whom the congregation supported because of their need. Others consider the list to include widows whom the congregation chose as deaconesses or at least
for some kind of similar service. Without in advance choosing one or the other explanation, let us see what Paul says
about putting widows on the list.

There is an age requirement. Widows below the age of sixty are not to be enrolled. Paul will have more to say about
them later.

For what purpose were those above sixty enrolled? If they
were "real widows" at that age level, it is possible that it was
to provide for their support. So we can ask: Was this list perhaps a list of those widows above sixty who had no one to
support them and so were enrolled as the responsibility of the
congregation? That appears to be a possibility.

These enrolled widows, however, were also to have certain qualifications. They were to be such who had been

faithful to their husbands, who were well known for their good deeds. They were known to be good mothers. They were such who had shown hospitality, even washing the feet of fellow Christians ("saints") when they received them as guests. This was a service required after traveling by foot on paths, a service that generally was the task of servants. These were widows who had shown themselves adept at helping those in trouble, whom the troubled felt free to approach, and who willingly extended a helping hand. Paul had set up similar lists of qualifications for elders and deacons. So now we ask whether the list of qualifications shows that these widows were to serve the congregation in some special way, perhaps akin to the deacons. This, too, appears to be a possibility.

What about the younger widows? Does Paul contradict himself in what he says of them? They should not be put on the list because they may later want to marry and in doing so "bring judgment on themselves." But a few verses later Paul counsels the "younger widows to marry."

It appears that enrolling younger widows could become a temptation to them, especially if this meant that they would receive their full support from the congregation. Being still young and having considerable leisure time, they might yield to "their sensual desires." No longer dedicated to Christ, they might fall into a sinful life style in which marriage had no other purpose than to satisfy their desires. This might even result in their breaking "their first pledge [literally, 'faith']," thus bringing judgment on them. They would also be tempted to "go about from house to house," to "become idlers . . . gossips and busybodies, saying things they ought not to." In verse 15 Paul shows that he is basing what he writes on experience: "Some have in fact already turned away to follow Satan."

If enrollment on the list involved performing specific duties, these may not have been of such a nature that widows over sixty would be overburdened, nor that younger widows would be completely occupied. Some commentators have also proposed the thought that enrolling may have called for a "pledge" to dedicate the rest of one's life to the prescribed duties and not to marry again. For this reason the younger should not be enrolled. Since no such pledge is hinted at in the case of elders and deacons, one wonders why it would be required of enrolled widows. That a pledge of celibacy was required, the breaking of which would be considered worthy of judgment, seems unlikely. This was a later development in the Roman Catholic Church.

What is Paul's advice to the younger widows? He counsels them to marry, not simply to satisfy "sensual desires," but "to have children, to manage their homes." No one will be able to slander them with false accusations of immoral conduct or of being busybody gossips. This does not exclude the possibility that "real widows" who were still younger would temporarily receive help from the congregation, although they would not be enrolled on the list of widows. Another marriage must have been a viable prospect for younger widows. Paul advises them to follow this route with all the responsibilities it would place upon them. They would not become the permanent burden of the church with the temptations this exposed them to.

We have not found a definitive answer as to what it meant to put widows on the "list." Perhaps the answer includes something of both proposed explanations. Those on the list were recognized as the permanent responsibility of the congregation. They may also have been assigned service to the church that older widows with the stated qualifications could capably and best render.

16If any woman who is a believer has widows in her family, she should help them and not let the church be burdened with them, so that the church can help those widows who are really in need.

Having discussed the matter of placing widows on the "list," Paul again takes up the subject of their support. Believers should take care of the widows within their own families. This will enable the church to use its resources to provide for those widows who are "really in need." Different times and economic and social conditions may change how these principles are put into practice, but the role of caring concern by both family and church does not change. Let believers and the church not become indifferent and close their eyes to those in need.

Elders

17The elders who direct the affairs of the church well are worthy of double honor, especially those whose work is preaching and teaching. 18For the Scripture says, "Do not muzzle the ox while it is treading out the grain," and "The worker deserves his wages."

Timothy is to instruct the congregation at Ephesus not only about the qualifications of elders as he did in chapter three. He is also to teach the members about their responsibilities toward the elders. He writes about the elders who do their work well, but he also recognizes that sometimes elders may need to be rebuked.

We do not know how many elders there were at Ephesus. Paul speaks of them in the plural, as a group. They may have served in a team ministry with various elders having different assignments.

Some of them directed the affairs of the congregation. Elders were also called "overseers." If a group of Christians is to live together as a congregation, someone must "oversee" or direct its affairs. God wants his people to worship and work together in an orderly manner (1 Corinthians 14:40). There is need for good administration. We, too, need those who "direct the affairs of the church."

Ultimately everything the congregation does is in the interest of the gospel, God's holy word. Thus Paul especially mentions those elders "whose work is preaching and teaching." The apostles, too, considered the "ministry of the word of God" their primary task (Acts 6:2). Of the many duties a pastor may be expected to fulfill, nothing should interfere with teaching and preaching. Many activities that take place within the church may be useful and beneficial, but only of God's word can it be said that the church cannot exist without it.

Elders who do their work "well" are "worthy of double honor." Whether work is "well" done can be determined only according to God's standards and not those of man. People may be pleased to hear what their itching ears desire to hear (2 Timothy 4:3), but only what corresponds to God's eternal truth is well taught, well spoken. Only conduct that agrees with God's holy will is well done. The pastoral letters provide a standard by which to judge.

Those who serve in the public ministry should not seek honor, fame, acclaim or material benefits. They will carry on their work faithfully, humbly, knowing that any success is the work of the Lord. Only as he blesses can they succeed. Nevertheless, God does not prohibit the church from acknowledging work well done. Rather, those who serve the church should receive honor and respect, "doubly" so when they do their work well. "Double honor" hardly is to be thought of in mathematical terms, as receiving exactly twice as much honor as one whose work is not done as well. The word used for honor has the idea of value in it. Faithful ministers are to be valued and treasured highly.

The two quotations that follow show that Paul wants the congregation to show honor also by properly providing for the material needs of those who serve. "Do not muzzle an ox while it is treading out the grain" is quoted from Deuteronomy 25:4. The oxen who were used to trample out the grain on the threshing floors were not to be muzzled to prevent their eating some of the grain. The Apostle Paul quotes this passage in 1 Corinthians 9, applying it to himself and his fellow missionaries: "Is it about oxen that God is concerned? Surely he says this for us, doesn't he? . . . If we have sown spiritual seed among you, is it too much if we reap a material harvest from you?" (9:9-11).

The other quotation is from Jesus as recorded in Luke 10:7: "The worker deserves his wages." Luke's gospel was written prior to 1 Timothy and we can assume that Paul was acquainted with it. Jesus applied these words to the support that the men he sent out to preach were to receive. Paul summed it up as follows: "The Lord has commanded that those who preach the gospel should receive their living from the gospel" (1 Corinthians 9:14).

Thus the manner in which the church provides for those who serve well is a way of showing honor. Put into today's terms, by the salary it pays and the benefits it provides, a congregation shows honor and respect for its called workers. It hardly shows "double honor" if their support is kept at the poverty or minimum subsistence level. Neither should the pastor expect, however, that "double honor" requires that those he serves make him a man of wealth.

¹⁹Do not entertain an accusation against an elder unless it is brought by two or three witnesses. ²⁰Those who sin are to be rebuked publicly, so that the others may take warning.

Elders too were still sinful, fallible human beings. They too fell into sin. They too might prove unfaithful. Since they were serving in a public office, they might, however, be subject to criticism according to the likes and dislikes of one or the other member. To carry out Christian discipline, to deal properly with elders who had sinned and to avoid individual criticism from being brought before the congregation, Paul advises Timothy: "Do not entertain an accusation against an elder unless it is brought by two or three witnesses." In carrying out Christian discipline it is important that "every matter may be established by the testimony of two or three witnesses" (Matthew 18:16; cf. Deuteronomy 19:15).

Paul knew from personal experience that it would not be possible to please everyone. He personally experienced false accusations. He knew that those who serve in the public ministry will be subject to careful scrutiny. They may be accused falsely by individuals who don't like what the pastor or teacher is doing. Only accusations supported by the testimony of witnesses should be considered.

When an accusation against an elder has been duly established, rebuke is in order. This should be administered "publicly," literally "before all." The assumption is that the sin, too, was a public matter, since there were at least two or three witnesses.

The purpose for the public rebuke is "so that others may take warning." Who are the "others"? Some take this to refer to other elders. It would seem rather that the "others" is a broader reference to fellow Christians in general. If a pastor sins and is corrected publicly, this will serve as a warning to the entire congregation. To attempt a "cover-up" will serve neither the called worker nor the people. Because their work is of a public nature, public rebuke is in order. If, however, the sin is so private that it is known only to the sinning pastor and the one who rebukes him, the eighth commandment will prevent making it public.

Pastors are to be examples to the flock in their faith and life. When their sin requires public rebuke, let them also be an example in repentance. Let them not seek to excuse or hide their sin. Let them humbly accept the rebuke and confess. Let them turn to the Lord for forgiveness. Let them produce the fruits of repentance. And let them humbly accept whatever may be the consequences of their sin "so that others may take warning."

Further Instructions

[21]I charge you, in the sight of God and Christ Jesus and the elect angels, to keep these instructions without partiality, and to do nothing out of favoritism.

Favoritism has no place in the church. Also elders when they sin (cf. verse 20) should not receive more favored treatment than others in the congregation. God treats all sinners alike, condemning all, and sending Christ as a Savior for all. "In the sight of God and Christ Jesus," who is fair toward all, Paul solemnly charges Timothy to be equally impartial.

Who are the "elect angels" in whose sight Paul makes this charge? We do not know for certain. A possible answer is that he is referring to the holy angels, the "elect" angels in contrast to those who fell away (Jude 6; 2 Peter 2:4). These holy angels are in the presence of God and God uses them as his messengers to serve Christians (Hebrews 1:14).

Pastors may be tempted to have "special" friends in the congregation. They may provide pastoral care with greater concern to members they like than to others who are not as close to them. Congregations may give preferential treatment to a prominent member, a man of wealth or a generous contributor. They may show partiality in the choice of elders and deacons. "Do nothing out of favoritism" is not only good advice but a solemn charge of the apostle.

22Do not be hasty in the laying on of hands, and do not share in the sins of others. Keep yourself pure.

Laying on of hands was done in healing the sick (Acts 28:8), in bestowing a blessing (Mark 10:16), in giving the Holy Spirit (Acts 8:17-19), in conferring an office (Acts 6:6: 13:3; 1 Timothy 4:14). In this context Paul no doubt has reference to the last of those mentioned, to conferring a congregational office like that of elder or deacon.

Timothy is not to be hasty in conferring an office on anyone. If he failed to assure himself of the individual's qualifications and Christian conduct, Timothy would show an indifference toward sin. He would share responsibility for the sins committed by the individual while in office and for the damage such conduct might do to the church. This reminds us of Paul's earlier prohibition against investing a "recent convert" as overseer (3:6). What Paul says here has broader application, having in mind not only the newly converted. If a congregation becomes careless in choosing its leaders, responsibility for the misconduct and sins of poorly chosen leaders is shared by the congregation. We are responsible not only for what we ourselves do, but for what we condone in others. "Keep yourself pure" by not sharing in the sins of others.

23Stop drinking only water, and use a little wine because of your stomach and your frequent illnesses.

Some believe that Timothy took Paul's warning against drunkenness and intemperance (3:3,8) so to heart that he drank only water. We don't doubt that Timothy must have known about Jesus' first miracle when he provided wine for the wedding of Cana. He must have known the Psalm that speaks of the plants God causes to grow which provide also "wine that gladdens the heart of man" (Psalm 104:15). It therefore is doubtful that he drank only water because he was a "prohibitionist." But he may have wanted to set a good example for those who were tempted to overindulge. It may also have been his personal preference.

Whatever the reason, Paul advises him to "use a little wine" for the sake of his health. Was Timothy's stomach perhaps especially sensitive to impurities in water? Whatever Timothy's "frequent illnesses" were, wine could serve a beneficial purpose. Paul's attitude toward drinking alcoholic beverages is one that does not reject moderate use, but without equivocation rejects their abuse as sin.

24The sins of some men are obvious, reaching the place of judgment ahead of them; the sins of others trail behind them. 25In the same way, good deeds are obvious, and even those that are not cannot be hidden.

Some people sin openly so that their actions must be condemned even before they themselves are brought to judgment. Their sins reach "the place of judgment ahead of them." Such people may pride themselves in that they are not hypocritical about their sin, trying to hide it. Avoiding hypocrisy, however, does not justify committing sin.

On the other hand, those who cover up their sins under hypocrisy will be found out eventually. Their sins may "trail behind them," but, if not before, in the Lord's judgment they will be exposed by him who knows all things.

The same is true of good works. Some are open and evident and by their very nature may be seen. Jesus himself says to his followers: "Let your light shine before men, that they may see your good deeds and praise your Father in heaven" (Matthew 5:16).

This does not mean, however, that the one who does them should strive for recognition. The Lord also warns: "Be careful not to do your 'acts of righteousness' before men, to be seen by them" (Matthew 6:1). The one who does the good deeds is not concerned with being seen by men. Nevertheless, sooner or later, the deeds will become evident; they cannot be hidden. If not before, in the final judgment the Lord will point to the good works as evidence of faith (Matthew 25:34-40).

In writing these verses Paul may still have had in mind what he said about not laying hands on anyone hastily. Timothy is not to share in the sins of others through haste in judging their qualifications. He must carefully look at what is evident, their sins and their good deeds. Time will help him more clearly to recognize the one or the other. Therefore the requirement not to act hastily. This does not, however, call for a cross-examination and careful investigation into the secrets of anyone's life. Some things will remain hidden until the time of the Lord's judgment. The church cannot act on the basis of what the Lord will reveal in his own good time.

Slaves and Masters

6 All who are under the yoke of slavery should consider their masters worthy of full respect, so that God's name and our

teaching may not be slandered. [2]Those who have believing masters are not to show less respect for them because they are brothers. Instead, they are to serve them even better, because those who benefit from their service are believers, and dear to them. These are the things you are to teach and urge on them.

Slavery was part of the social and economic structure within the Roman Empire. It has been estimated that within Rome itself about a third of the population was slaves, some of them cultured and well educated. That the gospel found acceptance among slaves is seen from Paul's frequent reference to them in his letters. Paul wrote a letter to Philemon, whose run-away slave had become a Christian. He bade Philemon to receive Onesimus as a brother in Christ. There must have been slaves enough in the Ephesian congregation so that Paul has special instructions to Timothy about them.

Repeatedly, Paul expressed the thought that "there is neither slave nor free," that we "are all one in Christ Jesus" (Galatians 3:28). Slaves who recognized the spiritual freedom they had in Christ might conclude that this applied to all earthly relationships. From what Paul writes we may conclude that some slaves were tempted to despise heathen masters and to treat even their Christian masters with less respect because they were their brothers in Christ.

Paul held no brief for slavery. Earlier in this letter he had listed "slave traders" with "adulterers and perverts . . . liars and perjurers" and "whatever else is contrary to the sound doctrine" (1:10). Paul also did not inaugurate a crusade simply to abolish slavery in the Roman Empire or in the world, desirable as that might have been. Rather, he shows how the gospel will have its effect on Christians as they live in the slave and master relationship.

Slaves with heathen masters should consider them "worthy of full respect, so that God's name and our teaching may not be slandered." When a slave is a Christian, his conduct toward his heathen master brings honor or shame on Christ and the gospel. If the slave shows no respect, Christ will as a result be blasphemed among the heathen. If slaves have believing masters, that is all the more reason, not for disrespect, but for even better service "because those who benefit from their service are believers, and dear to them,"

In his letter to the Ephesians Paul speaks at greater length to the slaves. They are to obey their earthly masters "just as you would obey Christ. Obey them not only to win their favor when their eye is on you, but like slaves of Christ, doing the will of God from your heart" (Ephesians 6:5,6). Peter adds the point that this willing service and respect is to be rendered "not only to those who are good and considerate, but also to those who are harsh" (1 Peter 2:18).

Paul has no separate instructions to Timothy regarding the masters. Of course, what he writes in his letter to the Ephesians concerning masters applies also here, namely that Christian masters are to "treat your slaves in the same way" (Ephesians 6:9), that is, with respect and love, reflecting faith in Christ. Thus the gospel as it converts sinners can profoundly affect and change undesirable customs and practices that may be present in a sinful world.

The relationship of a worker to his supervisor differs from that of a slave toward his master since the worker remains a free person. Yet much that is said in this section can also find application in a society that prohibits slavery. Christianity does not abolish relationships in which one person is in a position of authority over another, but it will affect how Christians function in those relationships.

Paul again reminds Timothy of his teaching responsibility at Ephesus: "These are the things you are to teach and urge on them." What Paul writes to Timothy is intended to help him profitably and correctly teach others. This applies to what he just wrote, to everything in the letter, also to what follows.

A Description of False Teachers

3If anyone teaches false doctrines and does not agree to the sound instruction of our Lord Jesus Christ and to godly teaching, 4he is conceited and understands nothing. He has an unhealthy interest in controversies and quarrels about words that result in envy, strife, malicious talk, evil suspicions 5and constant friction between men of corrupt mind, who have been robbed of the truth and who think that godliness is a means to financial gain.

Paul's concern for "sound instruction" included repeated warnings against false teaching. This was a matter of deep concern to Paul. For the third time he takes up this subject (cf. 1:3ff; 4:1ff). The church can ill afford an indifferent attitude "if anyone teaches false doctrines."

False doctrine can be recognized in that it "does not agree to the sound instruction of our Lord Jesus Christ and to godly teaching." What our Savior taught, whatever is recorded for us in Holy Scripture, is the sole basis for judging anyone's teaching. Anything that contradicts or does not agree with what Jesus taught is false. He taught that he alone is the way to the Father (John 14:6), and that way is pure grace. "It is by grace you have been saved" (Ephesians 2:8). False teaching always in some manner promotes salvation by works, that man can and must do something to gain God's favor. It adds a condition we must fulfill—"if you keep the commandments" —"if you accept Jesus into your life"—"if you avoid certain foods"—"if you do your best"—even "if you believe," making faith a contributing work on our part. Such false conditions are not "sound," healthy teaching that can heal the troubled heart. It is not "godly teaching" that leads to true godliness in living.

"He is conceited and understands nothing" is Paul's further description of the false teacher. What conceit it is to say: "Lord Jesus, I know more than you. I will follow my own ideas and not what you teach." Such a person, though he may have received numerous educational honors, in fact "understands nothing." In his conceit he displays his ignorance by not listening to Jesus, by placing himself above Holy Scripture.

The false teacher "has an unhealthy interest in controversies and quarrels about words." False teachers are not satisfied to reject Christ's teaching only for themselves but want to convince others to join them in their errors. They no longer let words mean what they say. Words become a field of battle. A patent example is the Jehovah's Witnesses. In their zeal to make proselytes, they base their arguments on a misinterpretation of the words and grammar of Scripture that is reflected in their own, often erroneous, Bible translation. For example, since they deny the divinity of Christ, they translate John: "Originally the Word was, and the Word was with God and the Word was a god" (not God with a capital G).

The way of the false teacher leads to "envy, strife, malicious talk, evil suspicions and constant friction between men of corrupt mind." False teaching creates dissension and division in the church and among Christians. How different this is from the peace, love, joy, comfort and hope that come through Jesus' sound teaching.

"Who have been robbed of the truth"—among the false teachers are also such who at one time knew the truth. No church nor individual can afford to become smug or complacent about possessing true doctrine. Whoever does not fight the good fight of faith may find himself misled, deceived and robbed of the truth that was once cherished.

False teaching is also prone to use its false "godliness" as "a means to financial gain." The greed of the human heart cannot resist using even "godliness" for gain. At the time of the Reformation the Roman church had turned the false "godliness" of indulgences into a source of fabulous riches. What wealth the "godliness" of an Oral Roberts, and of others, has amassed via the mass media is well documented. In truth, we all have hearts that are easily seduced by the desire for wealth. So we find Paul continuing with a warning about the love of money.

Those Who Desire Riches

6But godliness with contentment is great gain. 7For we brought nothing into the world, and we can take nothing out of it. 8But if we have food and clothing, we will be content with that. 9People who want to get rich fall into temptation and a trap and into many foolish and harmful desires that plunge men into ruin and destruction. 10For the love of money is a root of all kinds of evil. Some people, eager for money, have wandered from the faith and pierced themselves with many griefs.

Paul had just pointed out that it was wrong to make "godliness" a source of riches. Now he says that godliness is "great gain." Is he contradicting what he just said? Not at all, he is speaking here of true godliness. True godliness is faith in the Lord Jesus together with the kind of life that faith produces. This brings contentment, the opposite of dissatisfaction and greed. The world would arouse the latter; the Lord works the former.

Job, a man of wealth, lost everything he had. Yet he could say: "Naked I came from my mother's womb, and naked I will depart. The LORD gave and the LORD has taken away; may the name of the LORD be praised" (Job 1:21). Paul echoes the same thought: "For we brought nothing into the world, and we can take nothing out of it." The Christian, knowing that earthly possessions are a gift of God for this life only, can say: "May the name of the Lord be praised for the much or little I have." That is true contentment. And that is gain.

What Paul writes can also lead to a proper recognition of life's true needs. "But if we have food and clothing, we will be content with that." The word for "clothing" literally means "covering" and includes not only what directly covers the body but also shelter. Food and covering satisfy our basic needs. When God provides these, there can be contentment. Paul showed such a spirit of contentment when he wrote: "I know what it is to be in need, and I know what it is to have plenty. I have learned the secret of being content in any and every situation" (Philippians 4:12). Thus faith speaks. Thus godliness is associated with contentment.

Whoever bases his hope and sense of security on riches will never be content. Such a person seeks to gain ever more, to the very end of life. The Christian finds his security in the Lord's promise: "Those who seek the LORD lack no good thing" (Psalm 34:10). The Lord Jesus says: "So do not worry, saying, 'What shall we eat?' or 'What shall we drink?' or 'What shall we wear?' For the pagans run after all these things, and your heavenly Father knows that you need them. But seek first his kingdom and his righteousness, and all these things will be given to you as well" (Matthew 6:31-33). What greater gain is there than to have this promise of the Lord?

Yet people want to get rich. Christians too are tempted. The desire for riches, however, is beset with dangers. "People who want to get rich fall into temptation and a trap and into many foolish and harmful desires that plunge men into ruin and destruction." In how many lives that are controlled by a desire for riches have not events followed a familiar course: yielded to temptation, trapped in a sinful course, driven to foolish and senseless actions, lost in ultimate ruin? This course of events may not always be outwardly evident. The rich man "who was dressed in purple and fine linen and lived in luxury every day" seemed to have everything going for him. That he had succumbed to the temptations of riches and was trapped in a life style that would lead to ruin did not become evident until he died and found himself in hell (Luke 16:19-31).

Money itself is not the evil. The Lord made Abraham a wealthy man. Most Christians are blessed with more money than is needed to supply a minimum of food and covering. Christians may even be granted great wealth and serve God with it. Paul writes that it is "the love of money" which is "a root of all kinds of evil." The attitude the heart takes toward wealth becomes the root problem. To love money, to be "eager for money," leads to all kinds of evils. The rich young man, even though he lived a virtuous life, loved his wealth and turned away from Christ. Judas loved money and betrayed his Lord and in grieving despair took his own life. "Some people, eager for money, have wandered from the faith and pierced themselves with many griefs." What a contrast: contentment under God's promises versus greed that leads to ultimate ruin!

Charge to Timothy

¹¹But you, man of God, flee from all this, and pursue righteousness, godliness, faith, love, endurance and gentleness. ¹²Fight the good fight of the faith. Take hold of the eternal life to which you were called when you made your good confession in the presence of many witnesses.

Paul calls Timothy a "man of God." In doing so he is not setting him apart from other Christians, as though what Paul is writing applies to him only because he is a pastor. "Man of God" applies to all those referred to by Peter when he calls Christians "a people belonging to God" (1 Peter 2:9). Paul uses the term again in 2 Timothy 3:17 in the same sense of anyone who belongs to God, whom God thoroughly equips for every good work by means of his word. Naturally what applies to every "man of God" should be taken to heart particularly also by Timothy as a leader in the church and by those whom God calls into his special service.

"Flee from all this," that is, the desire to be rich and the temptations to which this leads, the love of money and all the evils associated with it. In the previous chapter (5:17,18) Paul had spoken of the financial responsibility the church has toward "those whose work is preaching and teaching." "The worker deserves his wages." In this present verse Paul warns against greed, also on the part of those in the public ministry. "Flee," keep on running away from "all this," in your heart and in your actions. No pastor, and no Christian, can "serve both God and Money" (Luke 16:13).

Rather, "pursue righteousness, godliness, faith, love, endurance and gentleness." As a "man of God" strives to live a righteous and godly life, as he seeks to grow in faith and love, as he patiently endures affliction and shows gentleness toward fellow sufferers, he will be fleeing the greed that looks only to self.

When a sinner is brought to faith, he is enlisted in a fight, "the good fight of the faith." When Paul spoke of fighting the good fight in chapter 1 (verse 18), he used a word in Greek that speaks of going to war and engaging in battle. Here he uses a word that refers to athletic contests, like the races and wrestling matches that were a part of the Grecian games. There is no essential difference, however, whether we speak of the Christian contest, race or battle. Scripture uses all of these expressions in referring to the Christian's ongoing struggle in this world against his flesh and Satan.

Timothy is to fight the good fight of faith. Faith consists in this that we "fear, love and trust in God above all things." It is believing the "trustworthy saying that deserves full acceptance: Christ Jesus came into the world to save sinners" (1 Timothy 1:15), that he "gave himself as a ransom for all men" (1 Timothy 2:6). Faith is putting one's "hope in the living God, who is the Savior of all men, and especially of those who believe" (1 Timothy 4:10). Faith builds on the full truth as revealed by God in Holy Scripture.

Whoever believes in the Lord Jesus is involved in a fight, for the devil "prowls around like a roaring lion looking for someone to devour." The Christian is called on to "resist him, standing firm in the faith" (1 Peter 5:8,9). Satan incites people to sins of all kinds, and sin is destructive of this saving faith in Christ. By false doctrine the devil seeks to lead people to place their trust anywhere else but in Christ and the saving gospel. Throughout this letter the theme of fighting the good fight of faith has been prominent as Paul instructs Timothy how he and those he serves may live godly lives and reject the false teachers and their destructive errors.

This call to fight the good fight of faith is, however, not a call to muster our own strength, to trust in our own powers. Relying on himself, Peter soon fell into shameful denial of his Lord. To the Ephesians Paul wrote how they may take their "stand against the devil's schemes." They are to "put on the full armor of God," all the weapons God gives for this fight. Paul names them: "the belt of truth . . . the breastplate of righteousness . . . the gospel of peace . . . the shield of faith . . . the helmet of salvation . . . the sword of the Spirit, which is the word of God" (Ephesians 6:11-17). Thus God equips us. The call to battle is the call to use the weapons God places into our hands, especially the sword of the Spirit, the word of God. When Satan attacks, cut him down with "it is written."

No wonder Paul is so concerned that faith persevere in this life-long struggle. By faith we "take hold of the eternal life." Not merely some temporal benefit like riches or honor and fame is at stake. Nothing less than eternal life, salvation, is the prize in this contest. Our Savior reminds us: "Whoever believes and is baptized will be saved, but whoever does not believe will be condemned" (Mark 16:16).

"To which you were called"—God brought Timothy to faith in the Lord Jesus by calling, inviting him through the gospel to receive eternal life. Through faith this gift is received, faith that the Spirit works in the sinner's heart by the gospel's call.

That Timothy believed was evident "when you made your good confession in the presence of many witnesses." This seems to refer to the time of Timothy's baptism, performed before many witnesses who, as was customary, heard his confession of faith. By his confession, one that was "good" according to sound doctrine, the faith God had worked in Timothy's heart showed itself. Eventually, these baptismal confessions grew into what we know as the Apostles' Creed.

At the time of their installation those who serve as pastors and teachers in the church make a "good confession." They confess and promise to teach only the inspired, inerrant Holy Scriptures. They promise to conduct their ministry in accordance with the church's published confessions, to live godly lives. Thus their teaching and living is to be an ongoing "good confession" made in the presence of many witnesses, the people whom they serve.

13In the sight of God, who gives life to everything, and of Christ Jesus, who while testifying before Pontius Pilate made the good confession, I charge you 14to keep this command without spot or blame until the appearing of our Lord Jesus Christ, 15which God will bring about in his own time—God, the blessed and only Ruler, the King of kings and Lord of lords, 16who alone is immortal and who lives in unapproachable light, whom no one has seen or can see. To him be honor and might forever. Amen.

"I charge you"—in the Greek text Paul begins verse 13 with these words. He is placing an important, solemn responsibility on Timothy. We can see how important it is as he makes this charge "in the sight of God . . . and of Christ Jesus." He is calling on them to witness what he is saying.

There are no greater witnesses. God is the one "who gives life to everything." He is the creator of heaven and earth, the source and giver of all life. Christ Jesus is the one "who while testifying before Pontius Pilate made a good confession." He testified that he was a king with a kingdom not of this world, that he bore witness to the truth (John 18:36,37). He testified to Pilate that he was the Son of God, as the Jews charged, over whom Pilate could have no power except it were given from above (John 19:11). Before these divine witnesses Paul makes his charge, for they are directly involved in what he is saying.

Timothy is "to keep this command without spot or blame." What command? Paul had just "commanded" Timothy to "flee from all this," the love of money and all the evils connected with it; rather to "pursue righteousness, godliness," etc. But "this command" is broader. He had also called on him to fight the good fight of faith. Can Paul have had anything less in mind than everything he has been "commanding" Timothy throughout his letter, not in the sense of placing him under any kind of law, but the Lord's command to teach and preach and live the full truth of the gospel and to train others for this same ministry? Nothing Timothy does should bring a "spot or blame" on the gospel work in which Timothy is serving under God's command. What an encouraging "charge" for this young leader of the church in Ephesus, one through which the Holy Spirit worked the very faithfulness it called for!

This should continue "until the appearing of our Lord Jesus Christ, which God will bring about in his own time." Timothy is to carry out his assignment with the thought ever before him that he wants to be judged faithful when the Lord returns. When that will be, neither Paul nor Timothy knew. Neither do we. God will bring about the return of Jesus "in his own time."

That Timothy would be alive at the time of Jesus' return is neither stated nor implied. All who are called into the Lord's service, in fact all Christians, should carry out the Lord's command, remembering that he is returning. Whether they are still alive on the last day or have died and been raised again, they will appear before the returning Lord. This charge to keep the Lord's command without spot or blame is one that every pastor, teacher, every Christian will take to heart until the day of the Lord's return. At his coming we will want to be adjudged faithful.

For a second time in this letter Paul sounds forth with a glorious doxology. The first time was when he wrote about Jesus' first coming to save sinners, of whom he was chief (1:17). Here he contemplates Christ's second coming and breaks out in a doxology that describes the glorious God who determines the appointed time for "the appearing of our Lord Jesus Christ."

He is "the blessed and only Ruler, the King of kings and Lord of Lords." It is as though Paul cannot find enough expressions to show the uniqueness, the "onliness," of our Ruler, Lord and King. There is no other like him. Of false gods there are many, but all these "gods of the nations are idols." Only the one true God "made the heavens" (1 Chronicles 16:26). The Muslims claim that Allah is that one true God: "There is no God but Allah." But any god who is not the Father of Jesus Christ, the one who was sent as the only Redeemer and Savior and will return at the appointed time, is an idol.

Implied in the term Ruler is the possession of all power. He is sovereign. This "only Ruler" is "blessed." All happiness and blessedness are personified in him, come from him, and are found only in his presence.

He "alone is immortal," not only that he will not die, but, literally, is "deathless." There is no such thing as death in him. He "has life in himself" (John 5:26). In his very essence and nature he is life. As mortals who must die, we have difficulty imagining or attempting to describe him who is "deathless." Even more difficult is it, however, to try to understand that Jesus Christ, who as true God was "deathless," yet took on our mortal nature, became man "so that by his death he might destroy him who holds the power of death—that is, the devil—and free those who all their lives were held in slavery by their fear of death" (Hebrews 2:14,15).

God "lives in unapproachable light," or, according to the Psalmist, "he wraps himself in light as with a garment" (Psalm 104:2). John simply states that "God is light; in him there is no darkness at all" (1 John 1:5). When John saw the heavenly Jerusalem he noted: "The city does not need the sun or the moon to shine on it, for the glory of God gives it light, and the Lamb is its lamp" (Revelation 21:23). So great is the brightness of the Lord's glory that when Moses requested to see it the Lord told him: "You cannot see my face, for no one may see me and live" (Exodus 33:18-20). Thus Paul writes of this "unapproachable light, whom no one has seen or can see." In his grace, however, this glorious God has revealed himself to us in his Son who says: "Anyone who has seen me has seen the Father" (John 14:9). Through him we will one day bask in that glory as it gives light to us during the eternal day in the heavenly Jerusalem.

As we reflect on who our God is and what he has done for us, we cannot but say with Paul: "To him be honor and might forever. Amen."

The Rich

17Command those who are rich in this present world not to be arrogant nor to put their hope in wealth, which is so uncertain, but to put their hope in God, who richly provides us with everything for our enjoyment. 18Command them to do good, to be rich in good deeds, and to be generous and willing to share. 19In this way they will lay up treasure for themselves as a firm foundation for the coming age, so that they may take hold of the life that is truly life.

In verses 6-10 Paul had spoken about material possessions. He encouraged contentment and warned against the temptations into which those who want to get rich fall and against the love of money as the root of all kinds of evil. But God may grant riches to Christians. In these verses Paul advises Timothy what he is to "command those who are rich," not in the sense of a legal prescription to earn salvation but as a guide for their Christian living.

Riches pose two dangers to the Christian. One is pride. "Command those who are rich in this present world not to be arrogant." In the world, the size of their bank account can determine people's status and how they feel about themselves. Let the Christian guard against this spirit of the world. Furthermore, let the church take care not to foster pride by showing partiality toward the rich. James warns against giving special attention to the person who comes "into your meeting wearing a gold ring and fine clothes" and discriminating against the poor (James 2:1-4). Paul had impressed on Timothy "to do nothing out of favoritism" (5:21). This includes favoritism that may be shown toward the rich. In Christ there is neither rich nor poor. All have the same promise and are equally rich.

The other danger for the rich is "to put their hope in wealth." The world considers wealth a major basis for security, but wealth "is so uncertain." A major catastrophe, an accident, a stock market crash, a costly illness can quickly wipe out earthly riches. The rich fool put his hope in his accumulated wealth but found how little security it gave him when God said: "You fool! This very night your life will be demanded from you. Then who will get what you have prepared for yourself?" (Luke 12:20).

What should Timothy tell those Christians "who are rich in this present world"? Like everyone else, they should "put their hope in God." Also wealthy Christians should remember that it is God "who provides us with everything for our enjoyment." As Christians they know that all things, they, their life, their possessions come from God.

Paul mentions God's purpose: "God provides us with everything for our enjoyment." God has created and preserves the world and all in it for us to use and enjoy. Scripture does not teach that a godly life is one of ascetic self-denial that considers as sin every use of God's gifts for pleasure.

Paul wants Timothy to direct wealthy Christians to derive enjoyment from their riches, enjoyment that is shared, enjoyment that can reach beyond this life. "Command them to do good, to be rich in good deeds, and to be generous and willing to share." Wealth brings little joy to the Christian if it becomes for him an opportunity for sin and is used selfishly. To be rich in earthly goods but poor in good works brings no true joy. Christians should learn the joy of generosity, the pleasure of sharing. "It is more blessed to give than to receive" (Acts 20:35).

The joy of having shared extends into eternity. "In this way they will lay up treasure for themselves as a firm foundation for the coming age, so that they may take hold of the life that is truly life." Jesus said: "Use worldly wealth to gain friends for yourselves, so that when it is gone, you will be welcomed into eternal dwellings" (Luke 16:9). Does this mean that when our money is used to perform good works they help us gain heaven? Never! Scripture unmistakably teaches salvation by grace alone without any works on our part. Paul is speaking of such who already have salvation by grace through faith. He is speaking of fruits that reveal the presence of faith. On the day of judgment the Lord will say to those at his right:

Come, you who are blessed by my Father; take your inheritance, the kingdom prepared for you since the creation of the world. For I was hungry and you gave me something to eat, I was thirsty and you gave me something to drink, I was a stranger and you invited me in, I needed clothes and you clothed me, I was sick and you looked after me, I was in prison and you came to visit me (Matthew 25:34-36).

Yes, what we did with our money, the good we did with it for others, the gifts to the poor, the concern for the helpless, the support of gospel messengers, will be recognized by our Lord as he bids us enter a blessed eternity. Be "rich in good deeds," not to earn heaven, but because that is the way faith is. It loves, it shares, it gives unselfishly. It shows what God has made you, an heir of heaven.

We can be sensitive about anyone telling us what to do with money. Should a pastor ever talk about this? Especially to those who are rich? Paul's answer is: "Command them to do good, to be rich in good deeds, and to be generous and willing to share." Yes, Paul is speaking also to today's Timothys. What we do with God's gifts is God's concern, and God's servants have the duty to tell us. Let the wealthy, and the not so wealthy, gratefully accept such instruction.

CONCLUSION: GUARD YOUR TRUST
1 TIMOTHY 6:20,21.

[20]Timothy, guard what has been entrusted to your care. Turn away from godless chatter and the opposing ideas of what is falsely called knowledge, [21]which some have professed and in so doing have wandered from the faith.

Grace be with you.

Paul concludes as he began, with a call to preserve God's truth, with a warning against the errorists. The truth, the gospel, must be preserved as a sacred trust and passed from generation to generation. The preoccupation of many already in the first generation of Christians with godless chatter and knowledge, falsely so called, shows how quickly Satan can beguile and mislead. Paul's advice is not: See what good you can find, what points of agreement; you can learn something from them also. His advice is simply: Turn away from them. Those who profess such teachings have wandered from the faith. That spells damnation. The danger and threat of error dare not be minimized.

Is Paul exaggerating? No, not when we remember that what is at stake is where people will spend eternity. The history of the church bears witness to the need for the warning. "Fight the good fight of the faith" is the call that sounds throughout his letter. Because of the deceptiveness of Satan, because of human pride and fickleness, let the church listen to Paul. Let its pastors and teachers and people carry on under God with fortitude and courage. The battle for the truth will not end until the Lord's return. Fight the good fight until he comes.

"Grace be with you." In the original, "you" is in the plural. Paul extends this closing wish not only to Timothy, but also to those with whom Timothy is expected to share the letter. It reaches down through the ages also to us. What a fitting conclusion!

> All depends on our possessing
> God's abundant grace and blessing,
> Tho' all earthly wealth depart.
> He who trusts with faith unshaken
> In his God is not forsaken
> And e'er keeps a dauntless heart.
>   (TLH, 425)

2 TIMOTHY
INTRODUCTION

The sequence in our Bibles has 2 Timothy as the second of the pastoral letters. Chronologically, however, it is the third. In fact, this is the last of all the letters written by the Apostle Paul.

For the second time Paul is a prisoner in Rome. This time he is not living in his own rented quarters, readily accessible to his friends. He is a prisoner in chains, suffering for the gospel (1:8,16). When Onesiphorus came to Rome, he had to search hard to find Paul (1:17). Paul's first appearance in court had not gone well, so he faces the imminent prospect of a martyr's death (4:6). For a more complete description of the historical setting and date of 2 Timothy, see the introduction to the pastoral letters (pp. 1-5).

Paul, the senior pastor and missionary, is for the last time writing to his very dear "son in the faith," a man he had personally chosen as his junior associate, a man who had worked so faithfully at his side and had been sent on various missions. This letter is more personal than was the first. There is less instruction about how the affairs of the congregation are to be conducted.

Why did Paul write this letter? He had some personal needs. Paul was lonely. Some of his associates had deserted or left him; others he had sent on missions. Only Luke was with him. He urged Timothy to come "quickly" and to bring Mark with him (4:9-12). When Timothy came, he should bring Paul's cloak and some scrolls and parchments (4:13).

Did Paul perhaps need additional clothing because of the coldness and humidity of the prison, especially in winter? Was he without any copies of the Scriptures and longed to be able to read and reread them?

Even greater than Paul's concern for his personal needs was his concern for Timothy and the church. This was a farewell letter. Paul wanted to leave with his dearest friend and the Lord's church these words of encouragement in written form. How necessary they would be during the "terrible times in the last days!" Here are final words of encouragement also for the many Timothys who are called to serve while there is still a time of grace, and for the people of God whom they serve in these "last days of sore distress."

Outline of 2 Timothy

Theme: ENCOURAGEMENT IN TROUBLED TIMES

Opening greeting: 1:1,2
I. Don't Be Ashamed of the Gospel 1:3-18
    A. Timothy's Sincere Faith 1:3-7
    B. Testify without Shame 1:8-12
    C. Guard the Good Deposit 1:13,14
    D. Deserters 1:15
    E. Faithful Onesiphorus 1:16-18

II. Be Strong in Christ 2:1-26
    A. A Good Servant of Christ Jesus 2:1-7
    B. Remember Jesus Christ 2:8-13
    C. An Approved Workman 2:14-26

III. The last days 3:1-4:8
    A. Terrible Times 3:1-9
    B. Persecutions 3:10-13
    C. Continue in the Word 3:14-17
    D. Preach the Word 4:1,2

OPENING GREETING
2 TIMOTHY 1:1,2

1 **Paul, an apostle of Christ Jesus by the will of God, according to the promise of life that is in Christ Jesus,**
²To Timothy, my dear son:
Grace, mercy and peace from God the Father and Christ Jesus our Lord.

As customary, Paul names himself as author and calls himself an apostle of Christ Jesus. The Lord Jesus had sent him on his mission. It was "by the command of God our Savior and of Christ Jesus" that Paul was serving as an apostle, as he also had expressed it in his first letter to Timothy (1:1).

Here he attributes his apostleship to "the will of God." Paul served not simply in obedience to a divine command but recognized that everything that happened to him as an apostle, also his present imprisonment and imminent martyrdom, was "by the will of God." How important it is for us as Christians, in good times and in bad, to recognize God's will in our lives! How important it is, especially for pastors and teachers! With the submission of faith we pray, "Your will, O Lord, be done."

Paul's mission as an apostle of the Lord Jesus was "according to the promise of life that is in Christ Jesus." "The promise of life" is nothing else than the gospel. Think of John 3:16. God sent his Son so that whoever believes in him would have eternal life. "I have come that they may have life, and have it to the full," Jesus said of himself (John 10:10). Jesus' resurrection proclaims life. Because he lives, we also will live. Everything Paul did as an apostle was in harmony with the gospel of life in Christ Jesus. That is the heart and soul of a pastor's work. This is what people will look for in their called servants, that they serve according to the promise of life in Christ Jesus. If this is lacking, nothing else is of value.

Paul did not have any children; he was not married. Yet in Timothy he had a "dear son," one who was closer to him than a birth child. Through the gospel God enabled Paul to "give birth to" Timothy as his son in the faith. When parents not only give their children physical life, but through the gospel in word and sacrament (baptism) bring about their spiritual birth and continue to nourish them with the Bread of Life, bonds of love closer than a mere physical relationship are present. Children can say to their parents: "You not only gave us life on earth, but you led us to become children of God and to receive eternal life." Blessed are the parents and children where this relationship exists. Like Paul, parents will call upon God to bless their children with the grace, mercy and peace that comes from God alone and from our Lord Jesus Christ. See the exposition of 1 Timothy 1:2 for a fuller description of this triad of blessings.

Encouragement in Troubled Times

These were troubled times in which Paul was writing to his "dear son." Paul will describe them later in the letter. Once more he must encourage Timothy, but in his loneliness Paul also desires the encouragement which Timothy's presence can bring.

How important it is for Christians to serve one another in troubled times! But are there ever times on earth that are not troubled? Are there ever times when we do not need the comfort of the gospel from our fellow Christians?

DON'T BE ASHAMED OF THE GOSPEL
2 TIMOTHY 1:3-18

Timothy's Sincere Faith

³I thank God, whom I serve, as my forefathers did, with a clear conscience, as night and day I constantly remember you in my prayers. ⁴Recalling your tears, I long to see you, so that I may be filled with joy. ⁵I have been reminded of your sincere faith, which first lived in your grandmother Lois and in your mother Eunice and, I am persuaded, now lives in you also.

In prison Paul had much time to think. How easy it would have been to feel sorry for himself, how easy to begin to blame and complain. Paul rather thanks God. From his forefathers he had learned to serve the one true God as revealed in the Old Testament. When the Lord Jesus came, he revealed himself as the fulfillment of God's promises and called Paul into his service. God had turned Paul from a persecutor into a courageous witness and effective missionary. Rome treated him as a criminal. Even many of his fellow Jews had sought his life. But Paul had "a clear conscience." He was serving his Lord according to the Lord's will and direction.

In prison Paul also had much time for prayer. "Night and day" he remembered Timothy as he prayed. What an encouragement this was for his "dear son." Are we too busy to pray? And to pray for one another? Are pastors too busy to pray for their members? And members for their pastor? Sometimes, when we are ill or shut-in or in retirement, the

Lord "gives" us time to think and pray as never before. What looks like a time of uselessness can become a blessing to us and to those we remember in our prayers.

Paul cannot help remembering the tears he saw in Timothy's eyes, very likely the last time they parted. We do not know when this was or what the circumstances were. Had Paul perhaps said something to the effect that they would not see each other again? Separation brings sorrow. Paul is now hoping once more to experience the complete joy of being with Timothy. He mentions this again in chapter 4:9,21.

As Paul thinks of Timothy he also is reminded of Timothy's family. Eunice, Timothy's mother, was married to a Gentile. Timothy had not been circumcised as a child. Yet she followed the good example of her mother Lois's faith. Paul can speak of the sincere faith of both. They believed in the God who revealed himself in the Old Testament. When Paul came to Lystra proclaiming Jesus Christ as the promised Messiah, they believed. The Holy Spirit had worked a "sincere" faith in their hearts, one that showed itself also in the way they instructed Timothy in the Old Testament Scriptures when he was still a child (3:15). He too came to believe the Scriptures were fulfilled in Christ. So Paul had no doubt at all about the sincerity of Timothy's faith. We see how the godly examples of faithful parents and grandparents can bring eternal blessings to children and children's children.

⁶For this reason I remind you to fan into flame the gift of God, which is in you through the laying on of my hands. ⁷For God did not give us a spirit of timidity, but a spirit of power, of love and of self-discipline.

Because God had blessed Timothy in the past by working in him a sincere faith, "for this reason" Paul impresses on him to "fan into flame the gift of God." As Christians we cannot rest secure in the knowledge of blessings received in the past, a faith we have because of God's grace active in our lives in the past. We have the ever present need for the Spirit-filled word to fan the flame of faith to burn more brightly.

Paul again reminds Timothy of the special gift of God received when, with the laying on of hands, he was ordained into his pastoral office. He had referred to this also in 1 Timothy 4:14. Exactly what this gift was in Timothy's case we are not told. We can conclude that when the Lord invests us with special duties in his kingdom he also gives gifts to fulfill them. How often we see that a Christian pastor or teacher grows with the new responsibilities placed on him, as he conscientiously devotes himself to his teaching and preaching. Thus he fans into flame the gift of God.

Paul describes the kind of spirit God gave "us," that is, him and Timothy and the rest of his co-workers. It is not "a spirit of timidity," or cowardice and fear. Timothy appears to have been somewhat fearful by nature, timid because of his youth (see 1 Corinthians 16:10 and 1 Timothy 4:12). He needed this encouragement against timidity, and we all often need it in the face of a hostile world.

The spirit given by the Holy Spirit is one of "power, of love and of self-discipline." The Word of God is powerful and empowers Christians (Hebrews 4:12). Then the Christian sees in Jesus' love the perfect inspiration and pattern of love, and this power and this love are used with self-discipline, with moderation and prudence. What a marvelous spirit God gives "us" as we are called on to serve him and his holy people! What an encouragement for Timothy and for every pastor, teacher and Christian! While a young pastor will guard against false self-confidence, he need not labor with timidity and fear when he presents the truth revealed by God.

Testify Without Shame

⁸So do not be ashamed to testify about our Lord, or ashamed of me his prisoner. But join with me in suffering for the gospel, by the power of God, ⁹who has saved us and called us to a holy life — not because of anything we have done but because of his own purpose and grace. This grace was given us in Christ Jesus before the beginning of time, ¹⁰but it has now been revealed through the appearing of our Savior, Christ Jesus, who has destroyed death and has brought life and immortality to light through the gospel.

Having reminded Timothy of the kind of spirit God had given, Paul continues to encourage him. "Do not be ashamed to testify about our Lord, or ashamed of me his prisoner." One of two things can prevent unashamed testimony: (1) fear of a world hostile to Christ, or (2) failure to see Christ as one's "Priceless Treasure." Fear of Jesus' enemies made Peter ashamed to testify and caused him to deny his Lord. On the other hand, as long as Paul did not recognize Jesus as the Son of God and promised Savior, he not only failed to testify but even persecuted Jesus' disciples.

Timothy should not fear to join Paul in suffering for the gospel. Paul calls himself "his," that is, the Lord's prisoner. The Roman emperor might think that Paul was his prisoner. Not so, the almighty God is still in control. The Jews too thought they could make the apostles their prisoners. "But during the night an angel of the Lord opened the doors of the jail and brought them out"(Acts 5:19). King Herod was unable to keep Peter as his prisoner when the Lord determined otherwise (Acts 12). Confidently Timothy can join Paul in his suffering. What they are doing they do "by the power of God." There is no room for fear.

This God of all power is also a God of amazing grace. How is it that one should then be ashamed of him? He "saved us and called us to a holy life—not because of anything we have done but because of his own purpose and grace." What a clear, simple commentary of these words we have in *Luther's Small Catechism*. He "saved us"—"redeemed me . . . with his holy precious blood." "And called us"—"the Holy Ghost has called me by the gospel, enlightened me with his gifts, sanctified and kept me in the true faith." "To a holy life"—to "live under him in his kingdom, and serve him in everlasting righteousness, innocence and blessedness." "Not because of anything we have done," indeed, not even coming to faith was our doing—"I cannot by my own thinking or choosing believe in Jesus Christ, my Lord, or come to him." That is God's way. All this happened "because of his purpose and grace."

It is grace from beginning to end. Think of it. "This grace was given us in Christ Jesus before the beginning of time." Paul speaks more fully of this "glorious grace" to the Ephesians: "For he chose us in him before the creation of the world to be holy and blameless in his sight. In love he predestined us to be adopted as his sons through Jesus Christ, in accordance with his pleasure and will—to the praise of his glorious grace, which he has freely given us in the One he loves" (Ephesians 1:4-6). What God planned for me before I was born, yes, before the world was created, had to be by grace and nothing but grace.

What God "before the beginning of time" purposed and planned we cannot know unless he himself reveals it to us. This he did "through the appearing of our Savior, Jesus Christ." Even before man through sin had brought death on himself, God planned to send the Lord Jesus to destroy death. In Hebrews 2:14,15 we are told how he accomplished this: "Since the children have flesh and blood, he [Jesus] too shared in their humanity so that by his death he might destroy him who holds the power of death — that is, the devil — and free those who all their lives were held in slavery by their fear of death." There is still more to it.

The one who destroyed death also "has brought life and immortality to light through the gospel." That Jesus accomplished all of this is evident by his resurrection. Without the resurrection Jesus' death would have been a defeat, useless. There is no better commentary on this than the inspired one of Paul himself in chapter 15 of 1 Corinthians. You may wish to read the entire chapter. Here are several pertinent, choice verses:

> For what I received I passed on to you as of first importance: that Christ died for our sins according to the Scriptures, that he was buried, that he was raised on the third day according to the Scriptures, and that he appeared to Peter, and then to the Twelve. . . . But if it is preached that Christ has been raised from the dead, how can some of you say that there is no resurrection of the dead? . . . If Christ has not been raised, your faith is futile; you are still in your sins. . . . But Christ has indeed been raised from the dead, the firstfruits of those who have fallen asleep.

Through the prophets God had promised life and immortality. When God the Son "in the fullness of time" appeared on earth as a historical person this purpose was revealed in all its fullness and completeness. People could visibly observe Jesus and what God did to accomplish their salvation in him. "We have seen his glory," John could write (John 1:14).

117

Feed My Lambs

There is no question about what God, even before creation, had in mind for us. Only look at Jesus and you will know.

But Timothy wasn't there in person to witness Jesus' death and resurrection. Neither were we. How then can we know about life and immortality in Christ? About Jesus' saving work? We know "through the gospel." Thus the Lord Jesus has brought all this to light and continues to do so. Let no pastor, let no church member ever underestimate the importance of the enlightening power of the gospel.

[11]And of this gospel I was appointed a herald and an apostle and a teacher. [12]That is why I am suffering as I am. Yet I am not ashamed, because I know whom I have believed, and am convinced that he is able to guard what I have entrusted to him for that day.

Since the gospel is the means by which our Savior brings "life and immortality to light," he sees to it that it is heard. He appoints preachers, apostles, teachers. "And how can they believe in the one of whom they have not heard? And how can they hear without someone preaching to them? And how can they preach unless they are sent?" (Romans 10:14,15). Here as in 1 Timothy 2:7 Paul refers to his call as herald, apostle and teacher. The Lord God and none other had commissioned him to preach. This privilege and responsibility Paul pursued with single-minded devotion.

That is the very reason, Paul says, "why I am suffering as I am." He was in prison because he preached Christ. In the Rome of Emperor Nero that was a capital crime. "Yet I am not ashamed." The threat of martyrdom had not silenced Paul. His present imprisonment was not a disgrace. He had no reason whatsoever to be ashamed.

Why not? "Because I know whom I have believed, and am convinced that he is able to guard what I have entrusted to him for that day." Paul's faith had not been shaken. He knew exactly who Jesus was and what he had done for him. Nothing could shake his conviction that his trust in Jesus would not be in vain.

Commentators are not agreed on the translation and meaning of the last part of verse 12. The Greek words which here are translated "what I have entrusted to him" literally mean "my deposit." They could also be translated "what he entrusted to me." This writer prefers the NIV translation. What, then, is that "deposit"? What is it Paul had entrusted to the Lord Jesus? The following appears to be a likely meaning: Paul had entrusted himself and his entire salvation totally to Jesus. What he now had by faith the Lord Jesus would deliver to him in its complete reality on "that day," the day of his return. There would be no disappointment about this. Jesus would not fail him on that final day of redemption. His trust would be realized. To know Jesus "who has brought light and immortality to light" is to have this conviction. To know that one's salvation is safe in the hands of the Lord Jesus is not to look anywhere else for it. We too can have the firm conviction that on the final day the Lord will deliver what he has promised.

Guard the Good Deposit

13What you heard from me, keep as the pattern of sound teaching, with faith and love in Christ Jesus. 14Guard the good deposit that was entrusted to you — guard it with the help of the Holy Spirit who lives in us.

"Keep." "Guard." What is so important that Paul calls for such careful keeping? What must be guarded against loss and damage? Answer: the words which Timothy had heard from Paul. They were a "good deposit" which Paul had entrusted to Timothy, or rather, which God through Paul had entrusted to him. That is nothing else than the gospel, the word of God. This must be carefully kept and guarded. Why?

The reason is not simply to keep it in a safe place like a diamond in a safety deposit box. What Paul had entrusted to Timothy serves "as the pattern of sound teaching." Only if Timothy and those he would train used Paul's words as "pattern" for their teaching would it be "sound."

In these pastoral letters Paul repeatedly uses the word "sound" in reference to faith and teaching (1 Timothy 1:10; 6:3; 2 Timothy 4:3; Titus 1:9,13; 2:1,2). The word translated "sound" literally means "healthy." Like spoiled food, contaminated teaching will only be harmful. To benefit anyone Timothy's teaching must be "sound," healthy, correct according to a specific pattern.

The pattern of soundness was Paul's own teaching. Was Paul perhaps arrogant in setting up his words as the pattern? Not at all, Paul knew that he taught by special inspiration of God. It is the writings of Paul and the apostles, of the prophets and evangelists that are inspired and serve as an infallible "pattern." All teaching in the church and all mission work must follow this pattern. Therefore it must be guarded carefully. To lose the pattern is to lose the means that makes for healthy teaching.

Fortunately the guarding of this "good deposit" does not depend on mere humans. Left to ourselves with our natural human reason we would soon spoil everything. Only "with the help of," or better, "through the Holy Spirit who lives in us" is this guarding accomplished. The church indeed needs to pray: "Grant, we beseech Thee, Almighty God, unto Thy Church Thy Holy Spirit . . . that Thy Word, as becometh it, may . . . be preached to the joy and edifying of Christ's holy people, that in steadfast faith we may serve Thee and in the confession of Thy name abide unto the end."

121

Deserters

15You know that everyone in the province of Asia has deserted me, including Phygelus and Hermogenes.

In encouraging Timothy "not to be ashamed," Paul draws attention to the many who were not setting a good example in this. The province of Asia (today western Turkey) was the area where Paul had done much mission work. Its capital was Ephesus, where Timothy was serving as pastor. We might expect Christians from this province to come to Paul's defense. These were dangerous times, however, and they did not want to become involved. We don't know any details. They were known to Timothy. Phygelus and Hermogenes may be people whom one would least expect to desert Paul. Sometimes even the best of Christians or a trusted pastor prove disappointing.

Faithful Onesiphorus

16May the Lord show mercy to the household of Onesiphorus, because he often refreshed me and was not ashamed of my chains. 17On the contrary, when he was in Rome, he searched hard for me until he found me. 18May the Lord grant that he will find mercy from the Lord on that day! You know very well in how many ways he helped me in Ephesus.

Over against those who deserted Paul, Onesiphorus was a noble example of one who was "not ashamed of my chains." He had come to Rome. Since Paul was chained in a prison, Onesiphorus could not easily find and gain access to him. Onesiphorus was persistent, however. He searched until he found Paul. Repeatedly he came to see Paul and "refreshed" him. He may have supplemented the meager provisions for his bodily needs in prison, but especially he also refreshed

Paul spiritually by his very presence and words of reassurance. Timothy himself knew only too well "how many ways he [Onesiphorus] helped me in Ephesus." Onesiphorus had been a most precious brother in Christ.

Who knows how often a faithful member has been an "Onesiphorus" to his young pastor and helped him with words of encouragement. What a help it can be when an older pastor takes his young colleague into his confidence and helps him through difficult times. Yes, even the zeal of a young pastor may encourage an older pastor when he experiences disappointments.

Paul prays that the Lord may "show mercy to the household of Onesiphorus." Yes, the pious deeds of a God-fearing father bring blessings to the entire family. In addition, he prays for Onesiphorus, "that he will find mercy from the Lord on that day!" What a joy it will be to hear the Lord on the last day say to him: "Come, you who are blessed by my Father; take your inheritance, the kingdom prepared for you since the creation of the world." Then the Lord will point to the fruits of faith, "I was in prison and you came to visit me." When? "Whatever you did for one of the least of these brothers of mine, you did for me" (Matthew 25:34-40). What greater blessing could Paul desire for faithful Onesiphorus? What an encouraging example for Timothy, and for us!

BE STRONG IN CHRIST
2 TIMOTHY 2:1-26

A Good Servant of Christ Jesus

2 **You then, my son, be strong in the grace that is in Christ Jesus. ²And the things you have heard me say in the presence of many witnesses entrust to reliable men who will also be qualified to teach others.**

Not to be ashamed of the gospel and of Paul will require strength on the part of Timothy, moral and spiritual strength. Where can he find it? He can find it by looking not to himself but to Christ. He will find strength in the grace, the undeserved love, of God that is in Christ Jesus. Our gracious God gives strength as we listen to everything he has done for us in Christ.

Timothy must be strong, for he is an important link in the chain that provides for the "good deposit" to continue. "The things you have heard me say in the presence of many witnesses entrust to reliable men who will also be qualified to teach others." Timothy is to establish a worker training program for the church; he is to become a seminary professor. He is to teach future pastors and teachers.

The men he is to train as pastors are to have specific qualifications. Here Paul mentions two: faithful and qualified to teach. Whoever is to be given a trust must be faithful, trustworthy. Sound teaching is to continue from generation to generation. So these faithful men not only must be able to learn, but also be capable of teaching others.

Paul is calling on Timothy to establish a worker training program, like the one which Christ already carried out in training the Twelve. Let no congregation or church body fail to recognize the importance of this responsibility. Only as we continue doing what Paul tells Timothy to do will sound teaching and preaching continue.

The church must enlist its capable, gifted young Christians for pastoral and teacher training. It must provide a training that conforms to the pattern of "sound teaching." It must encourage those it trains to make faithful use of God-given gifts as they prepare "to teach others." "Therefore we want to cherish and support our theological institutions of learning and see to it that the professors are faithful men and capable teachers, above all, such who teach the pure, sound doctrine of the apostles" (Zahn).

This is the provision the Lord made for the future. The church must have a well-indoctrinated ministry which is also able to communicate the message well. Only when the church has such a ministry will it effectively fulfill its mission. Paul, the greatest missionary of all time, is here speaking under inspiration.

3Endure hardship with us like a good soldier of Christ Jesus. 4No one serving as a soldier gets involved in civilian affairs — he wants to please his commanding officer. 5Similarly, if anyone competes as an athlete, he does not receive the victor's crown unless he competes according to the rules. 6The hardworking farmer should be the first to receive a share of the crops. 7Reflect on what I am saying, for the Lord will give you insight into all this.

When Paul became a prisoner, there were those who deserted him, not willing to suffer with him. Not so Onesiphorus, and certainly not Timothy. Paul encourages his young co-worker to endure the hardships that are part of their ministry. In this world the church is an embattled church. Timothy is to think of himself as a soldier, a good one.

A good soldier serves his commanding officer with single-ness of purpose. He must avoid becoming entangled in civil-ian affairs. He cannot have divided loyalties. Those the Lord enlists as full-time workers in the church, as soldiers in his army, must be intent "to please" him who is their head. A pastor who holds down a "civilian" job to enrich himself is hardly a good soldier of Christ. It is true, Paul worked as a tentmaker, but he did so in the interest of the gospel. Like-wise, if a congregation cannot provide for the pastoral fami-ly, a tent, or shared, ministry may be arranged. To serve Christ with a singleness of mind also does not mean that a pastor will neglect his family. Indeed, he will be a good hus-band and father because this too is his responsibility under God and pleases the Lord.

In encouraging Timothy, Paul uses a second illustration, that of the athlete. If he expects to receive the crown he must "compete according to the rules." Recently in the Olympics a runner who had come in first lost the gold medal because he had used steroids against the rules. The Lord Jesus sets up the rules for pastors and teachers. They are to "preach the gospel." The pastor who neglects to preach the crucified Christ and instead becomes politically active or who engages simply in social reform is in danger of losing "the victor's crown." "To compete according to the rules" is to do the will of the heavenly father, to follow "sound" doctrine, as the apostle puts it.

A third illustration as encouragement to Timothy pictures the "hardworking farmer." Here Paul is not telling Timothy what to do, but rather the blessings he can expect from his hard and difficult work. "The hardworking farmer should be the first to receive a share of the crops." We might ask by way of application: How does a pastor receive the first fruits of his work? These are not financial or earthly benefits, although the Lord promises those also. The fruits of the pastor's labors are spiritual, for his work is to sow the seed of God's word. His members will receive spiritual fruits from his faithful preaching. However, as the pastor studies the word and prepares a sermon or Bible study, he will reap a rich harvest of fruit for himself in spiritual growth, in a strengthened faith, in comfort and joy through Christ. The sermon a pastor prepares for his people he first preaches to himself.

Paul concludes these illustrations with this advice: "Reflect on what I am saying, for the Lord will give you insight into all this." He calls for meditation on Timothy's part and on ours. This advice applies for all of God's word and to all of God's people. As we reflect on God's revelation, the Lord sends the Holy Spirit who enlightens us to understand it more fully. What a pleasant surprise we may have when the Lord gives us understanding we didn't have before. This is the reward of study and meditation.

Remember Jesus Christ

8Remember Jesus Christ, raised from the dead, descended from David. This is my gospel, 9for which I am suffering even to the point of being chained like a criminal. But God's word is not chained.

Timothy, every pastor and teacher, every Christian must always remember whom he is serving. This is particularly important when service includes suffering such as Paul was experiencing. To "remember Jesus Christ" is to remember and serve someone who was "raised from the dead," who is alive. It is to "remember" and serve the one who "descended from David." His descent identifies him as the promised Messiah, a king of royal blood, who entered this world as a true human being, in whom dwells all the fullness of the Godhead bodily.

Paul identifies Jesus Christ with the gospel he preached. It is this gospel, he says, "for which I am suffering even to the point of being chained like a criminal."

Was this the end of the gospel? Far from it. We can almost hear Paul shouting out the next words: "But God's word is not chained." The preaching of God's word does not depend on any one person. God will see that it continues, as he has promised. Through his church he will continue to call pastors and teachers to proclaim his name throughout the world according to his will. This is true also today when the world seeks to intimidate "sound" preachers with ridicule and scorn.

10Therefore I endure everything for the sake of the elect, that they too may obtain the salvation that is in Christ Jesus, with eternal glory.
11Here is a trustworthy saying:
If we died with him,
we will also live with him;
12if we endure,
we will also reign with him.
If we disown him,
he will also disown us;
13if we are faithless,
he will remain faithful,
for he cannot disown himself.

"Therefore," because the word of God is not bound, Paul says, "I endure everything." Paul's suffering and imprisonment would be intolerable if that meant the end of the gospel,

128

of its freely being preached. But that is not the case. So he can endure everything, because the gospel continues unbound, still wins victory after victory.

Paul is not thinking of himself and feeling sorry for himself. He is thinking of those who are still benefiting from the gospel. The "elect" are all those whom God chose in eternity, who have been or will be brought to faith in the Lord Jesus Christ. They will be preserved in that faith through the word and finally "obtain the salvation that is in Christ Jesus, with eternal glory." For their sake Paul endures everything. In him they can see that the way to glory leads through suffering. Paul was an example of what he taught, that "our present sufferings are not worth comparing with the glory that will be revealed in us" (Romans 8:18). What an encouragement Paul offers to fellow Christians by his patience and endurance while suffering affliction and persecution for the sake of the gospel!

Paul now recites a "trustworthy saying" that further shows the relationship between suffering and glory. From the way he introduces the saying, "Here is a trustworthy saying," (in Greek simply, "trustworthy the saying"), it seems that Paul is referring to a saying familiar to Timothy. Its form is poetic, each verse containing a condition and conclusion. The condition states the circumstances under which the conclusion follows, not necessarily a condition we must fulfill to gain or earn what follows in the conclusion.

When did we die with Christ? What does it mean to live with him? Paul gives the answer to these questions in Romans 6:2-11. He tells us that we were "buried with him [Christ] through baptism into death." With him our "old self was crucified." Thus joined to Christ and his death by faith, we also live with him now in newness of life. And we share in his resurrection unto life eternal in heaven. By baptism, by the faith we there receive, we have a part in Christ's death and resurrection.

The Christian's life in this world calls for endurance. Jesus said: "All men will hate you because of me, but he who stands firm to the end will be saved" (Mark 13:13). To Christians in the face of persecution the living and exalted Lord says: "Be faithful, even to the point of death, and I will give you the crown of life" (Revelation 2:10). Those who wear crowns are kings, and so the Lord says of them that "they will reign forever and ever" (Revelation 22:5). What a glorious prospect! What an encouragement for patience in suffering!

There is a corresponding warning: "If we disown him, he will also disown us." This echoes Jesus' own words: "Whoever disowns me before men, I will disown him before my Father in heaven" (Matthew 10:33). Even those who render Christ lip service during Sunday worship may deny him by their ungodly lives during the week. Jesus said: "Not everyone who says to me, 'Lord, Lord,' will enter the kingdom of heaven, but only he who does the will of my Father who is in heaven" (Matthew 7:21). Those who have served only with their lips will hear the fearful words of Jesus on the day of judgment: "I never knew you. Away from me, you evildoers!" (Matthew 7:23). As pastors, as Christians, we must take care lest ungodly lives deny him whom we with our lips claim as our own. The pastor's life is a sermon that either confesses Christ or denies him.

"If we are faithless," what then? Will the Lord also then become faithless toward us? Not so. Never. The Lord ever remains faithful to his promises. "He cannot disown himself." He would not be God if he were to become unfaithful. Paul writes to the Romans: "What if some did not have faith? Will their lack of faith nullify God's faithfulness? Not at all! Let

God be true, and every man a liar" (3:3f). "Jesus Christ is the same yesterday and today and forever" (Hebrews 13:8).

Does this mean that it really doesn't matter much if we are faithless? By no means, let the unbeliever, let whoever turns from faith to unbelief, let whoever denies Christ by his ungodly life be warned. A faithful God remains true to his word, also his word of judgment: "Whoever does not believe will be condemned" (Mark 16:16).

It nevertheless remains a comfort and an encouragement to know that God remains faithful. To disown God and reject his grace in unbelief will indeed result in rejection. But God invites the sinner to repent, to return. When the sinner does, he will find the same grace and forgiveness from which he had turned. It remains and is there for the returning prodigal. Luther applies this to our baptism: "If anybody falls away from his baptism let him return to it. As Christ, the mercy-seat, does not recede from us or forbid us to return to him even though we sin, so all his treasures and gifts remain. As we have once obtained forgiveness of sins in Baptism, so forgiveness remains day by day as long as we live" (Large Catechism). Those who have become faithless, a pastor (shepherd) will seek to bring back; he will "go to look for the one [sheep] that wandered off" (Matthew 18:12).

An Approved Workman

14Keep reminding them of these things. Warn them before God against quarreling about words; it is of no value, and only ruins those who listen.

Timothy is to continue reminding the "reliable men" he is training of "these things." What things? Everything Paul is writing to him, particularly what he has just said about the Lord Jesus. Timothy is to continue doing what he has been doing. Good teaching involves more than saying something once. What scripture proclaims about Christ and our salvation must be taught and retaught. Here is something that Timothy, and we, must not tire of teaching and hearing when training pastors, and they in turn, when they serve the members in their congregations.

Already in his first letter Paul had warned Timothy against "quarrels about words" (6:4). Timothy is to pass this warning on to those he teaches. This is not a warning against careful word for word study of Holy Scripture, especially in the original languages. There is a quarreling about words that is unprofitable, however, that does not build up but tears down faith, that "only ruins those who listen." Often false teaching has its beginning in such quarreling about words, taking them out of context and putting new meanings into them. This quarreling appears to have happened in Ephesus. This practice must be rejected, and God's word be allowed to speak for itself, according to its clear meaning and sense.

15Do your best to present yourself to God as one approved, a workman who does not need to be ashamed and who correctly handles the word of truth.

Timothy, like every pastor and teacher, is one of God's workmen. He will do his best to meet with God's approval. He will want to pass the test.

When does one of God's workmen not need to feel ashamed? When can also a Christian congregation "approve" of its pastor? They can when he "correctly handles the word of truth." The word used in the original literally means "to cut straight." Applied to the word of truth it means to handle it correctly. In studying and applying God's word we must "keep things straight." We must approach the word with integrity, go straight to what it plainly says. The word of truth must not be changed to what appeals to human reason, e.g., regarding creation, sin, grace, moral standards.

We must also apply the word correctly, as God wants it applied. That too is "keeping things straight." We must apply the law to expose sin and work contrition. "By the law is the knowledge of sin" (Romans 3:20 KJV). We must proclaim the gospel to comfort the sinner with complete and full forgiveness according to the riches of God's grace in Christ. To speak the comfort of the gospel to the hardened sinner is to "throw your pearls to pigs" (Matthew 7:6). To preach the law to the despondent sinner is to drive him to despair. In either case one does not "correctly handle" the word of truth. The physician must prescribe the right medicine according to the condition of the patient. Similarly, the pastor is to apply the word of truth correctly according to the needs of the sinner.

16Avoid godless chatter, because those who indulge in it will become more and more ungodly. 17Their teaching will spread like gangrene. Among them are Hymenaeus and Philetus, 18who have wandered away from the truth. They say that the resurrection has already taken place, and they destroy the faith of some. 19Nevertheless, God's solid foundation stands firm, sealed with this inscription: "The Lord knows those who are his," and, "Everyone who confesses the name of the Lord must turn away from wickedness."

What the errorists were saying must be avoided, for it is nothing but godless chatter, profane and empty talk. They may speak about god, but what they say is godless, for it does not speak of the true God. Their vain speculations lead them ever farther from God, and they become the more godless, both in what they say and in their life and conduct. Such godless chatter must be avoided because its teaching "will spread like gangrene." It is appealing to human pride and vanity. However, it must be recognized for what it is, as dangerous as a malignant growth, which, left unchecked, spreads and eats away at healthy tissue and bone with lethal results. Let no pastor, let no Christian fail to recognize the destructive nature of false doctrine. Even as a cancer is destructive of physical health, so the godless chatter of errorists destroys spiritual health.

Paul does not hesitate to name names. Hymenaeus he had mentioned already in his first letter together with Alexander (1:20). Here he adds Philetus. What we know of him is limited to this reference. These men had wandered from the truth and had destroyed the faith of some. They must be named, lest their claim to Christianity hide their true identity. At times a pastor may need not only to describe a destructive error, but to name individuals or church bodies who spread this spiritual gangrene.

Paul refers to a specific error of which the men he names were guilty. "They say that the resurrection has already taken place." Certainly, for the Christian there is a resurrection that has already taken place, when those who were dead in sins are made alive in Christ (Colossians 2:13). Paul writes: "Since, then, you have been raised with Christ, set your hearts on things above" (Colossians 3:1). What these false teachers were saying, however, was not to affirm this spiritual resurrection, but to deny that there is a bodily resurrection. In 1 Corinthians 15 Paul clearly shows that a denial of the resurrection of the body is a denial of Jesus' bodily resurrection, and to deny that is to deny Jesus' saving work. "And if Christ has not been raised, our preaching is useless and so is your faith" (verse 14). What these false teachers were saying was destroying the very gospel Paul was proclaiming.

It was also very deceptive. The false teachers appeared to be teaching the resurrection, while in effect denying it. They used the same expressions as Paul, yet meant something else. That continues to be one of the deceptive ploys of those whose teaching destroys the gospel. The Mormons refer to Jesus Christ as Savior, yet deny his atoning death whereby he saves. The Jehovah's Witnesses refer to Jesus as "Son of God" yet deny that he is indeed true God. Also today there are those who speak of Jesus' resurrection and yet question whether his body ever left the tomb. There are those who speak of the Bible as God's word and as being truthful and yet deny its inerrancy. Such a crafty use of language must be exposed for what it is, and soundly rejected.

Although these false teachers "destroy the faith of some," Paul reassures Timothy: "Nevertheless, God's solid foundation stands firm." What does this refer to? There have been many explanations. We know that in 1 Timothy 3:15 Paul speaks of "the church of the living God, the pillar and foundation of the truth." This leads us to conclude that the holy Christian church, consisting of all believers, is the solid foundation that stands firm. These false teachers and their errors will not destroy it, though they may mislead some.

The inscription with which the "foundation" is sealed also shows it to be the church. "The Lord knows those who are his." Paul calls this the seal, giving certainty to what he is saying. God ever continues to gather his true believers, whom he had chosen in eternity. They will not be deceived (Matthew 24:24). Thus we confidently confess that "one holy Christian church will be and remain forever" (Augsburg Confession. Article VII).

Paul identifies a further seal: "Everyone who confesses the name of the Lord must turn away from wickedness." When Peter had confessed the name of the Lord, Jesus told him that "on this rock [Peter's confession] I will build my church, and the gates of Hades will not overcome it" (Matthew 16:18). Christians do not remain hidden. Though we cannot see faith in the heart, this faith leads to confessing the name of the Lord and to a life that turns away from wickedness. The power of the gospel will ever give evidence of itself in the church. The gospel as it is preached and confessed will reveal the presence of the church and show where it is being built. This will continue to the end of time, and Satan himself and all his hosts will not prevent it. Be reassured: "God's solid foundation stands firm" in spite of the errorists. God will see to it.

20In a large house there are articles not only of gold and silver, but also of wood and clay; some are for noble purposes and some for ignoble. 21If a man cleanses himself from the latter, he will be an instrument for noble purposes, made holy, useful to the Master and prepared to do any good work.

Comparing the church to a "large house," Paul pictures the church as we encounter it in this world. In it are articles of gold and silver, but also articles of wood and clay. In the visible church there are teachers and members who are instruments "for noble purposes," others "for ignoble." Clearly Hymenaeus and Philetus belonged to the latter.

What is he who "confesses the name of the Lord," who is an article of gold and silver, to do? He is to cleanse himself from "the ignoble." Cleansing has the purpose of removing oneself from the filth that wants to attach itself. The false teachers must be exposed, repudiated and excluded. Thus one proves to be an "instrument for noble purposes, made holy," that is, consecrated to the Lord. He renders useful service to his Master and is "prepared to do any good work." Paul goes on to describe some of this "good work" that is evident in the instruments for noble purposes.

²²Flee the evil desires of youth, and pursue righteousness, faith, love and peace, along with those who call on the Lord out of a pure heart. ²³Don't have anything to do with foolish and stupid arguments, because you know they produce quarrels. ²⁴And the Lord's servant must not quarrel; instead, he must be kind to everyone, able to teach, not resentful. ²⁵Those who oppose him he must gently instruct, in the hope that God will grant them repentance leading them to a knowledge of the truth, ²⁶and that they will come to their senses and escape from the trap of the devil, who has taken them captive to do his will.

"Flee the evil desires of youth." David prayed in the Psalm: "Remember not the sins of my youth" (25:7). Scripture sees the time of youth, when various desires emerge, as a time of special temptations for evil. This includes more than sexual desires, but also the desire for wealth, honor, power, position, pleasure, whatever form it may take. If Paul saw the need to warn his faithful co-worker and dear son in the faith (estimated to have been around forty at this time) against "youthful desires," certainly that warning is equally needed by young pastors today, and by those not so young. Do we ever fully outgrow those "evil desires"? The temptation to sin never ends. Many a pastor's career has been blighted and destroyed by yielding to sexual indiscretions, covetousness, pride, excessive drinking or the desire for a life of pleasure and ease. What Paul says in a special way to pastors is equally applicable to all Christians.

After this warning Paul encourages Timothy to "pursue righteousness, faith, love and peace, along with those who call on the Lord out of a pure heart." Similar encouragement was given Timothy in his first letter (6:11). For a more complete list of the fruits of the Spirit see Galatians 5:22,23.

In verse 23 Paul again warns Timothy against the errorists with their "foolish and stupid arguments." As he had written in his first letter (1:4), here too he points out that what they do produces quarrels. They produce quarrels, because what they say has to be opposed. Timothy cannot pursue peace with them by remaining silent. That would give the impression of agreement.

Paul continues by giving Timothy instructions on how to carry on polemics with those who oppose the truth. Let pastors, teachers and all Christians take to heart this instruction when they meet with opposition. "The Lord's servant must not quarrel" — don't let yourself in for a heated argument. "He must be kind to everyone, able to teach, not resentful." This is further explained in verse 25: "Those who oppose him he must gently instruct." Opposition readily raises resentment. Instead of instructing gently, with kindness, we begin to argue. There is a difference between teaching and arguing. Teaching seeks to give light and understanding. Arguing strives to overcome and win.

The pastor must remember that the purpose of talking with those who oppose him is "that God will grant them repentance leading them to a knowledge of the truth, and that they will come to their senses and escape from the trap of the devil, who has taken them captive to do his will." It is God, and not we with our clever arguments, who must lead them to repentance and to a knowledge of the truth. Not the errorist is the true opponent, but the devil who has taken him captive. Yet "gentle instruction" is called for, a clear, simple teaching of the truth. This, too, is part of correctly handling the word of truth.

This is Paul's description of an approved workman. Let every pastor and teacher listen and learn. May Paul's warnings and encouragements fall on receptive ears and hearts.

May the church pray for many such workmen who "need not be ashamed."

THE LAST DAYS
2 TIMOTHY 3:1-4:8

Terrible Times

3 **But mark this: There will be terrible times in the last days.** **2People will be lovers of themselves, lovers of money, boastful, proud, abusive, disobedient to their parents, ungrateful, unholy, 3without love, unforgiving, slanderous, without self-control, brutal, not lovers of the good, 4treacherous, rash, conceited, lovers of pleasure rather than lovers of God — 5having a form of godliness but denying its power. Have nothing to do with them.**

Paul wants Timothy to "mark," to "know," to "perceive," to "be certain of" the kind of world in which he and the church carry on their work. He describes what "people" (verse 2) will be like, that among them will also be such who have "a form of godliness" (verse 5), who still externally want to be known as Christians and belong to a church, go through the motions, and yet deny "its power." They reject its influence in their attitudes and conduct, which are like those of the people Paul describes.

Paul looks to the future, to what will be "in the last days." Quite naturally we think of the days preceding our Lord's return. Paul, nevertheless, tells Timothy to have nothing to do with the people he has described. What will be in the last days was already present at Paul's own time. These days had already begun. We can, however, expect that what he describes as being in the future will manifest itself ever more completely and fully as we move toward the day of Jesus' return. The "terrible times" will become ever more "terrible." Jesus himself had given a similar description (cf. Matthew 24).

What a description of the "last days" Paul gives! How closely it corresponds to the thinking and attitudes, to the philosophy of life promoted in the secular world today. What Paul here describes we also read in newspapers and hear on radio and see on television and sometimes experience among friends, associates and even in our families. The reader can fill in the details from his or her own experience as we briefly look at this description of the "terrible times."

"Lovers of themselves" — the "me first" and "I'm worth it" mentality.

"Lovers of money" — materialism, acquiring money becomes one's major concern.

"Boastful, proud" — not only as individuals but also as a society, confident that we can solve all problems given time, money and scientific research.

"Abusive" — literally, "blasphemers," speaking evil of God and ridiculing his word.

"Disobedient to their parents" — sometimes even encouraged by society and educators.

"Ungrateful" — whoever disobeys parents will also be ungrateful to them and enters into life with the idea that the world owes him or her a living.

"Unholy" — nothing is sacred, irreligious.

"Without love" — not even for family members.

"Unforgiving" — unwilling to be reconciled, contributing to the breakup of families.

"Slanderous" — literally "diabolical," making false accusations like Satan, the father of lies.

"Without self-control" — dissolute, exercising no restraint, for example, in drinking and sexual gratification.

"Brutal" — literally, "untamed," acting like savage beasts, even toward one's spouse and children.

"Not lovers of the good" — what is "good" is looked upon as unexciting, uninteresting, boring.

"Treacherous" — traitorous, willing to betray even a friend for one's own gain.

"Rash" — proceeding with no thought of others.

"Conceited" — blinded by an inflated self-esteem.

"Lovers of pleasure rather than lovers of God" — pleasure has become their god, hedonism, eroticism.

"Having a form of godliness but denying its power" — they still pretend to follow "religion" by going through the right motions, but they live as though God had no control and needed not to be taken into account. Although they may profess faith in God, they are practicing atheists.

Paul's advice to Timothy is, "Have nothing to do with them." This is sound advice not only to every pastor and teacher, but to every Christian. Paul is not calling on Christians to withdraw into monastic seclusion. They will still be in the world although not of the world. They will not join it in its ungodly philosophy of life, attitudes and conduct. Christians are to go into this world and be the "salt of the earth" and the "light of the world" (cf. Matthew 5:13,14) by living and proclaiming the good news of forgiveness and a new life in Christ.

6They are the kind who worm their way into homes and gain control over weak-willed women, who are loaded down with sins and are swayed by all kinds of evil desires, **7always** learning but never able to acknowledge the truth. **8Just as** Jannes and Jambres opposed Moses, so also these men oppose the truth — men of depraved minds, who, as far as the faith is concerned, are rejected. **9But** they will not get very far because, as in the case of those men, their folly will be clear to everyone.

Paul describes the treacherous manner in which some of the errorists ply their trade among the people they seek to mislead. "Weak-willed women" is not a description of women in general, but rather of the kind who are most easily misled by smooth and tricky arguments. Literally, they are "little women," with little will power. Evidently they have succumbed to sin, and their consciences are looking for relief. Their weakness of will also shows itself in being easily "swayed by all kinds of evil desires." They are controlled by their emotions, and we know that human emotions are no safe guide. Always seeking to learn, they fall for every new idea presented to them and never are "able to acknowledge the truth." The errorists Paul is describing "worm their way into the homes" of these women and gain control of them. One is sometimes surprised at the kind of control unscrupulous errorists can gain over others who fit Paul's description. We think of the control that some cults gain over their adherents in the name of religion.

These errorists "oppose the truth." They are not serving the true God. They are "men of depraved minds," evident in the vicious manner in which they prey on their victims. Even though they may claim faith, it does not stand the test of biblical scrutiny. Paul compares them to Jannes and Jambres, who opposed Moses. This is the only place in Scripture where these names are mentioned. Jewish tradition gives these names to two of the Egyptian magicians who opposed Moses before Pharaoh (cf. Exodus 7:11,22; 8:7). By their "secret arts" they were able for a time to imitate the miraculous signs Moses had performed with the power of God.

Paul holds out this comfort to Timothy regarding these deceivers. "They will not get very far because, as was the case of those men, their folly will be clear to everyone." It soon became evident that Jannes and Jambres could not stand up against the truth and power of God (cf. Exodus 8:18,19). Similarly the folly of these people will eventually expose itself to "everyone," not only to those guided by God's truth, but even to human reason.

Persecutions

10You, however, know all about my teaching, my way of life, my purpose, faith, patience, love, endurance, 11persecutions, sufferings — what kinds of things happened to me in Antioch, Iconium and Lystra, the persecutions I endured. Yet the Lord rescued me from all of them. 12In fact, everyone who wants to live a godly life in Christ Jesus will be persecuted, 13while evil men and impostors will go from bad to worse, deceiving and being deceived.

"You, however"—what a contrast there was between Timothy and the errorists and deceivers Paul had been describing! What a contrast between the way people would think and live and Paul's teaching and conduct! Timothy knew all about Paul's teaching and conduct. He had been Paul's prime pupil. He followed Paul as his Christian model.

The list that follows is impressive and can serve as a model for every pastor, teacher and Christian. In holding himself up as a model to know and follow, Paul is not bursting with pride and self-righteousness, but humbly and gratefully he recognizes what God has worked in him with his amazing grace.

"My teaching"—what Paul taught was God's inspired truth (cf. 1 Thessalonians 2:13).

"My way of life"—Paul's conduct showed the powerful influence of God's truth and agreed with his teaching. He practiced what he preached.

"My purpose"—Paul's life followed the plan and direction of God and so was not a meaningless serving of self.

"Faith"—it is described in Hebrews as "being sure of what we hope for and certain of what we do not see" (11:1).

"Patience" and "love"—the two go together. "Love is patient" (1 Corinthians 13:4). Patient love is vital for pastors and teachers in serving people. All Christians need it in their many human relationships.

"Endurance"—he is able to bear up under adverse and trying circumstances.

"Persecutions" and "sufferings"—Paul elaborates on these in the words that follow. He refers to incidents Timothy could well remember, since they happened in his native and neighboring cities: Antioch, from which Paul and Barnabas were expelled (Acts 13:50); Iconium, where there was a plot to stone them and from which they fled (Acts 14:5); and Lystra, Timothy's hometown, where Paul was stoned and left for dead (Acts 14:19). Paul gives a more complete list of his many sufferings to the Corinthians (2 Corinthians 11:23-29).

"Yet the Lord rescued me from all of them." In his letter to the Romans, Paul asked the question: "Who shall separate us from the love of Christ? Shall trouble or hardship or persecution or famine or nakedness or danger or sword?" (8:35). His confident answer, the result of his life's experience, was: "No, in all these things we are more than conquerors through him who loved us" (8:37). Yes, as a servant of the Lord even death is gain for him (Philippians 1:21). It is the final deliverance.

Paul was not an isolated case of persecution. As Timothy "followed" Paul in his teaching and conduct, he could expect the same kind of persecution. "In fact," writes Paul, "everyone who wants to live a godly life in Christ Jesus will be persecuted." Jesus had predicted this: "'No servant is greater than his master. If they persecuted me, they will persecute you also" (John 15:20). This does not mean that we must seek persecution, or conduct ourselves in a way that antagonizes. Paul sought to "become all things to all men so that by all possible means I might save some" (1 Corinthians 9:22). Yet persecutions came, because of Christ. So it will ever be when Christ is preached and lived. Let the Christian not consider this an evil. The early Christians in their persecutions rejoiced "because they had been counted worthy of suffering disgrace for the Name" (Acts 5:41).

The lot of the wicked and impostors, however, will be one that goes "from bad to worse." They will continue to deceive and as they do so they will also be deceived. The devil, the father of lies and deception, has them in his power, even to the point of Satan worship. Let whoever is involved in error and wickedness be warned that it is progressive, it goes "from bad to worse."

Continue in the Word

14But as for you, continue in what you have learned and have become convinced of, because you know those from whom you learned it, 15and how from infancy you have known the holy Scriptures, which are able to make you wise for salva-

Let the Little Children Come to Me

tion through faith in Christ Jesus. ¹⁶All Scripture is God-breathed and is useful for teaching, rebuking, correcting and training in righteousness, ¹⁷so that the man of God may be thoroughly equipped for every good work.

In contrast to the "evil men and imposters," who are deceivers and being deceived, Paul again (as in verse 10) emphatically addresses Timothy, "But as for you." Again, what a contrast! The deceivers go from bad to worse, but not so Timothy. You rather must "continue in what you have learned and have become convinced of." Timothy had learned well. He had acquired strong convictions. He should stand by them and not let himself be shaken from them. That is also the only way to resist and overcome the evil men.

To cling tenaciously to acquired convictions, however, is not necessarily a virtue. Sometimes we must give up long cherished convictions. Luther had to give up many "convictions" he had gained in his youth. So Paul gives reasons why Timothy should "continue."

"Because you know those from whom you learned it." Timothy had had reliable teachers. Who were they? For one, Paul himself. Earlier Paul had referred to "the things you have heard me say in the presence of many witnesses" (2:2). There were also Timothy's grandmother Lois and his mother Eunice. Paul had spoken highly of their "sincere faith" (2 Timothy 1:5). No doubt because of their instruction Paul could remind Timothy that "from infancy you have known the holy Scriptures."

Yes, we are to remember our leaders who spoke the word of God to us, and we are to imitate their faith (Hebrews 13:7). We do well to continue in what we have learned from Luther, from Walther, from Hoenecke, from the Piepers, from Meyer, from a faithful pastor who instructed us, from God-fearing parents who first brought us to Christ. Because we know those from whom we learned, we are to continue in what they taught us. May it also be said of our children that they from infancy learned the holy Scriptures from us!

This, however, is not simply a matter of tradition. It is not a matter of saying, "What was good enough for my parents is good enough for me." We do not blindly follow those who taught. Paul had a reason to exhort Timothy to follow those who had taught him. Through them he learned the holy Scriptures. This determines whether we have faithful teachers. Those who teach the word of God and are known for their sincere faith are worthy of emulation. Thank God if that is the kind of parent and teacher you have had. Continue in what they taught you, "because you know those from whom you learned it." The church needs faithful pastors, teachers, parents, Christians who can be models for succeeding generations.

Everything depends at last on faithfulness to the word of God. We must know the holy Scriptures. Why? They "are able to make you wise for salvation through faith in Christ Jesus."

The Scriptures Timothy had known since infancy were the writings of the Old Testament. From them he already had been brought to faith in the Christ, the promised Messiah. Jesus too had said of them that they "testify about me" (John 5:39). When Paul came to Lystra and showed that Jesus had fulfilled all promises regarding the Messiah, Lois and Eunice and Timothy believed. This was not a new and different faith, but they now knew the identity of the one in whom they already, on the basis of the Old Testament promises, believed.

What makes the Holy Scriptures so important is that they and they alone reveal the way of salvation, which is through faith in Christ Jesus. "As it is written: 'No eye has seen, no ear has heard, no mind has conceived what God has prepared for those who love him' — but God has revealed it to us by his Spirit" (1 Corinthians 2:9,10).

The Holy Spirit makes his revelation in and through the Scriptures. There is a close relationship between the Holy Scriptures and the Holy Spirit. "All Scripture is God-breathed." This makes the Scriptures unique. We call them divinely inspired. Peter also wrote about this: "No prophecy of Scripture came about by the prophet's own interpretation. For prophecy never had its origin in the will of man, but men spoke from God as they were carried along by the Holy Spirit" (2 Peter 1:20,21). God's Spirit brought about these writings. They were willed by God; God determined their content; the Spirit moved the writers to write in the way they did. The Scriptures truly are the very Word of God.

That "all Scripture" refers to the Old Testament here is beyond question. What about the New Testament? Paul claims such inspiration also for the apostolic writers. He writes to the Corinthians: "We have not received the spirit of the world but the Spirit who is from God, that we may understand what God has freely given us. This is what we speak, not in words taught us by human wisdom but in words taught by the Spirit, expressing spiritual truths in spiritual words" (1 Corinthians 2:12,13). Yes, God even taught them the very words in which to express his revealed truth. The Scriptures are verbally inspired. This is true of both the Old and New Testament writings.

These Scriptures are "useful." They thoroughly equip "the man of God," the pastor, teacher and every Christian "for every good work." For what are they useful? What are the good works for which they so completely equip us?

Paul first mentions "teaching." When Jesus gave his disciples the great commission to "make disciples of all nations," he said they should do this by "baptizing them" and by "teaching them to obey everything I have commanded you" (Matthew 28:19,20). This "everything" is what God has given us in the Holy Scriptures. They and they alone are "useful" for the kind of teaching we are to do.

The Scriptures are useful for "rebuking," that is, to expose, to reprove, to convict of sin. What is sin? Is abortion sin? Is sex outside marriage sin? Is drunkenness sin? Is divorce sin? Is failure to pay one's taxes sin? Not everyone gives the same answer. Who is right? The confusion in the world can also confuse the Christian. God determines what is sin. In Scripture God gives us the only reliable criterion on which to determine what is right and what is wrong. The Scriptures are useful for rebuking, for convicting the sinner of sin.

Scripture is useful for "correcting," that is, for restoring or improving those who fall. They need to be brought back to the straight and narrow way. The law rebukes, convicts; but to restore the sinner, the gospel is essential. The gospel moves the heart, strengthens faith, builds up so that correction takes place. Only holy Scripture proclaims the saving gospel, that leads us to Christ, without whom we can do nothing (John 15:5).

Finally, Scripture is useful for "training in righteousness." "Training" raises the picture of a child that needs to be disciplined and corrected, guided and encouraged if it is to grow up as a well-mannered useful citizen. Similarly the Christian during his life on earth needs ongoing training to attain to the righteousness of life (sanctification) that is part of being a Christian in this world of sin. The temptations of the flesh must be resisted. Satan continues to tempt. The Lord Jesus resisted the devil's temptations by responding with an "it is written." Yes, Scripture is useful "for training in righteousness," for it reveals to us the "grace of God that brings salvation," that "teaches us to say 'No' to ungodliness and worldly passions, and to live self-controlled, upright and godly lives in this present age" (Titus 2:11,12).

God has given us his holy, inspired, infallible, powerful Word, the Scriptures of the Old and New Testaments. Having this, a pastor and teacher, yes every Christian, is "thoroughly equipped for every good work" the Lord may ask of him. "Thoroughly equipped" means he has everything he needs to accomplish the task. Abraham said to the rich man, "They have Moses and the Prophets; let them listen to them" (Luke 16:29). When the rich man protested that someone rising from the dead would be more effective in leading his brothers to repentance, the answer was: "If they do not listen to Moses and the Prophets, they will not be convinced even if someone rises from the dead" (Luke 16:31). What a disaster if a pastor, or any Christian, neglects to use this divinely given equipment in favor of what is merely human and ineffective!

Preach the Word

4 In the presence of God and of Christ Jesus, who will judge the living and the dead, and in view of his appearing and his kingdom, I give you this charge: [2]Preach the Word; be prepared in season and out of season; correct, rebuke and encourage — with great patience and careful instruction.

After speaking about the usefulness of Holy Scripture in equipping "the man of God" for every good work, Paul gives Timothy a solemn charge to use that word in his ministry with diligence. This is an important matter, so he gives Timothy "this charge" "in the presence of God and of Christ Jesus." Thus he calls on them as witnesses, placing Timothy under oath before God to carry out the important assignment that is being given him. Paul is most serious about what he is enjoining Timothy to do.

In referring to Jesus Christ, he reminds Timothy that he is the one "who will judge the living and the dead." The Father "has entrusted all judgment to the Son . . . because he is the Son of Man" (John 5:22,27). Timothy is to do his work mindful that the Lord Jesus on the day of judgment will appear again as the glorious king he his. From him on that glorious day Timothy will want to hear the words, "Well done, good and faithful servant." In effect, Paul is making this charge to every "man of God," especially to every pastor and teacher to whom God has entrusted his sacred and effective word.

What is Timothy to do with the word? "Preach the Word." A preacher is a herald. A herald is vested with authority to proclaim publicly the official messages of a king or high official. The office of herald precludes permission to devise a message of his own. As one commentator describes preaching or heralding, "It is the earnest proclamation of news initiated by God. It is not the abstract speculation on views excogitated by man" (Hendriksen). Sermon writing, as well as preparing lessons for instructions and Bible classes, are challenging assignments for the pastor. He must communicate only the message his Lord has given him to proclaim. This, however, is not a command to do this in a dull, uninteresting, stereotyped manner. A clear and lively presentation shows the herald's concern that the Lord's message may be heard with understanding.

"Be prepared in season and out of season." Timothy should stand ready to serve as herald of the word at every opportunity the Lord presents. We recognize many opportunities as being "in season." Certainly that is true when the pastor stands in the pulpit on Sunday morning. The Lord gives other opportunities that to us may seem "out of season." It is important for us to be ready then, too, and not excuse silence with saying: "It was not the right time." On the other hand, this is not a command to be rude and overbearing in fulfilling this command or to force the word on those who clearly reject it. Jesus had something to say about that (Matthew 7:6; 10:14).

Let the pastor never find it inconvenient for himself to speak the word. The unbeliever and those who require admonition may look upon whatever time the pastor may wish to speak the word with them as "out of season." There is no "out of season" for the pastor, however, when the Lord says, "Speak." What we read in Proverbs, nevertheless, also is true: "A man finds joy in giving an apt reply — and how good is a timely word!" (Proverbs 15:23). A "timely word" is a word spoken at the right time. Sometimes circumstances may invite rejection. We trust the Lord to guide us. He even promises that in difficult situations the "Holy Spirit will teach you at that time what you should say" (Luke 12:12). So a pastor must preach and teach and keep on preaching and teaching.

As he preaches the word, Timothy is to "correct, rebuke and encourage." Only three verses before this, Paul had said that the word of God is useful "for rebuking." The same basic word is used here. To "correct" is to rebuke in the sense of exposing sin, of convicting of sin. The word translated "rebuke" in this verse adds to the thought of exposing sin also the idea of chiding and severely censuring someone for his sin. To "correct" and "rebuke" are both negative and by themselves will not cause a godly change. Timothy must "encourage," that is, with the gospel, he must free the conscience from sin and "from acts that lead to death, so that we may serve the living God" (Hebrews 9:14). Timothy must preach both law and gospel, the law to show the damage sin has done to us, the gospel to build us up with the love and mercy of a gracious God in Christ. The preacher must be able to say with Paul: "I have not hesitated to proclaim to you the whole will of God" (Acts 20:27).

"With great patience and careful instruction" Timothy is to do his preaching, rebuking and encouraging. Often we are tempted to look for quick results and give up when they aren't forthcoming. Let us rather strive to instruct with even greater care, explain things more clearly, and pray the Holy Spirit to open the heart of the hearer and bless the word according to God's promise. Should not the patience God has with us move us to "great patience" in our service of others?

Itching Ears

3For the time will come when men will not put up with sound doctrine. Instead, to suit their own desires, they will gather around them a great number of teachers to say what their itching ears want to hear. 4They will turn their ears away from the truth and turn aside to myths. 5But you, keep your head in all situations, endure hardship, do the work of an evangelist, discharge all the duties of your ministry.

"For the time will come" — this looks to the future, a future for which Paul wants to prepare Timothy. What Paul describes will begin even during Timothy's ministry but increase "in the terrible times in the last days."

Paul here distinguishes between what people need to hear and what they want to hear. What people need to hear is "sound doctrine." It is sound or healthy in that it says what God wants said. It comes from him, and it produces spiritual health.

The Blind Leading the Blind

People "will not put up with sound doctrine" because it does not say what they want to hear. It exposes their sin and proclaims condemnation. It does not flatter them with a recital of their great deeds and potential. When it proclaims deliverance from sin in the gospel, it does not make sense to human reason. An age that prides itself in man's great scientific accomplishments will not put up with the "foolishness" of "sound doctrine."

They will look for teachers who will "suit their own desires." By looking around long enough and going from teacher to teacher they will find "a great number of teachers," also within churches that call themselves Christian, who say what they want to hear. Their ears "itch" to hear what flatters their ego, what gives credit to man, what satisfies natural desires and lusts, what makes sense to human reason or doesn't make any sense at all but delights man because he has dreamed it up, what deifies man (humanism).

Instead of listening to the truth of "sound doctrine," they turn to "myths," referred to as "godless myths" in 1 Timothy 4:7. Paul may have been thinking of the Gnostic speculations that were beginning and became a threat in later generations. Ultimately, every false doctrine is a "myth." One is amazed at the "myths" to which people turn: the "myths" of Roman Catholicism: purgatory, salvation by works, invocation of saints, papal infallibility; the "myths" of theologians who reinterpret Scripture to correspond to human reason; the "myths" of evolutionism; the "myths" of astrology and other superstitions; the "myths" of Mormonism and the Jehovah's Witnesses; the "myths" of the "New Age" movement. The list is endless. Ears itch to hear anything except God's revealed truth. Every cult and religion, even every new and different misinterpretation of Scripture, find receptive ears in a world that has grown weary of the gospel, of "sound doctrine."

For a third time Paul emphatically addresses Timothy: "But you. . . ." Yes, Timothy, and this includes all pastors and teachers serving in the terrible times Paul describes, is to be different. "Keep your head in all situations," or "be sober," not meant literally of abstaining from wine, but that he should remain level-headed, keep a clear head. He must not permit himself to become confused or carried away in these situations. He must recognize and expose the "myths" for what they are. This will bring hardship on him. This he will endure. Also in these evil times he will "do the work of an evangelist." He will continue to follow Jesus' command to "preach the good news to all creation" (Mark 16:15). Timothy's assignment is to preach and keep on preaching the gospel. He must continue to "discharge all the duties of [his] ministry."

In a religiously confused world that will not put up with sound doctrine, it is vitally important that the church and its pastors remain sober, level-headed, and not succumb to the temptation to adapt their teaching to what people want to hear. Our teaching must be sound according to God's revealed truth. This good news we must proclaim and keep on proclaiming, whatever hardships we may experience. We never stop being evangelists. "Discharge all the duties of your ministry" is addressed to those the Lord calls into his service to the end of time.

Paul's Departure

6For I am already being poured out like a drink offering, and the time has come for my departure. 7I have fought the good fight, I have finished the race, I have kept the faith. 8Now there is in store for me the crown of righteousness, which the Lord, the righteous Judge, will award to me on that day — and not only to me, but also to all who have longed for his appearing.

Paul has repeatedly addressed Timothy personally and directly: "You, however . . . But as for you . . . But you" and solemnly charged him with urgent responsibilities. The reason is that the time of Paul's departure has come. Timothy will no longer have Paul to encourage and support him. Timothy must stand firm and be the support of others.

What thoughts must have gone through Timothy's mind and what feelings gripped his heart as he read Paul's words: "For I am already being poured out like a drink offering and the time has come for my departure." A "drink offering" in the Old Testament consisted in the pouring out of wine in connection with certain sacrifices (Exodus 29:38-42; Numbers 15:1-12). To be "poured out like a drink offering" may well be a reference to Paul pouring out his life in a martyr's death. The process that would lead to his martyrdom was already well along. When Paul wrote to the Philippians during his first imprisonment he also spoke of being "poured out like a drink offering" (Philippians 2:17). At that time he expected to be released (Philippians 1:25). This time, however, he says that the "time for my departure has come." Later in the chapter he speaks of his trial (verses16-18).

While the prospect of death is not terrifying to Paul, it does lead him to consider his past life and his ministry, which extended over a period of about thirty years. He had "fought the good fight." In admonishing Timothy he called it "the good fight of the faith" (1 Timothy 6:12). The fight of faith calls for resisting temptation and doing battle with those who would destroy the church and the gospel. Paul had "finished the race." In life's race Paul had not "run like a man running aimlessly" (1 Corinthians 9:26). He had written to the Philippians: "I press on toward the goal to win the prize for which God has called me heavenward in Christ Jesus" (3:14). In bidding farewell to the Ephesian elders

Paul had said: "I consider my life worth nothing to me, if only I may finish the race and complete the task the Lord Jesus has given me — the task of testifying to the gospel of God's grace" (Acts 20:24). Now with his approaching death that race was finished.

"I have kept the faith." Commentators are divided on whether Paul meant that he kept on believing or that he preserved the true faith, or sound doctrine. Of what value is believing, however, if it is not the truth which one believes? And of what value is the truth, if one does not believe it? The two go together. Paul had continued to believe and preserve the truth, "sound doctrine," as God had revealed it to him. God grant his church many pastors and many, many people who thus keep the faith!

As Paul faces death, what lies ahead? He is looking forward to "the crown of righteousness, which the Lord, the righteous Judge, will award to me on that day." The picture was one familiar to the Greeks. At the successful completion of a race, the victor received a wreath or crown. Paul anticipates the crown that the Lord will award him, having finished the race in accordance with God's will. The gospel testifies that this award is one of grace and not of works.

What is this "crown of righteousness" that Paul expects to receive from Jesus, the righteous Judge, on the day of his glorious return? It is a crown that consists of righteousness, a righteousness that at the Lord's coming would be Paul's.

Paul indeed already possessed the perfect righteousness of Christ, who fully kept the law. It was credited to Paul by faith. He wrote about it to the Romans: "This righteousness from God comes through faith in Jesus Christ to all who believe" (3:22). Paul had been set free from sin and had become a slave to righteousness (Romans 6:18). As such Paul said, "I have the desire to do what is good" (Romans 7:18).

Clothed in Christ's righteousness, Paul was a saint. Paul, however, saw "another law at work in the members of [his] body" (Romans 7:23). He still had an old Adam, his old sinful nature. He would do the evil that he as a Christian did not want to do. Yes, in his conduct and life he still was a sinner.

At Christ's appearance this will change. This present world of sin will be destroyed, "but in keeping with his promise we are looking forward to a new heaven and a new earth, the home of righteousness" (2 Peter 3:13). There we shall serve our God "in everlasting righteousness, innocence and blessedness, just as he has risen from death and lives and rules eternally," as Luther says in the explanation to the Second Article. We will be privileged to wear a glorious crown of righteousness, we who already now are clothed in the white robe of Jesus' righteousness. What a wonderful crown will be ours in the glories of heaven!

With longing anticipation Paul is looking forward to this glorious award. Not only he, it will be given "also to all who have longed for his appearing." To the Philippians Paul writes about us who are waiting: "We eagerly await a Savior from there [heaven], the Lord Jesus Christ, who by the power that enables him to bring everything under his control, will transform our lowly bodies so that they will be like his glorious body" (3:20,21). John looks forward to the glorious change that will take place: "Now we are children of God, and what we will be has not yet been made known. But we know that when he appears, we shall be like him, for we shall see him as he is" (1 John 3:2).

The Lord promises three crowns to those who remain faithful unto death. At his appearing he will give them "the crown of life" (Revelation 2:10), "the crown of glory" (1 Peter 5:4) and "the crown of righteousness," that Paul is here looking forward to as he faces death. It will be wonderful to live in glory, forever with Christ and all the saints, who in everything they think and say and do will be holy like Christ. What a wonderful prospect, after reading the description of the terrible times in the last days on this sinful earth! That is why believers say, "Amen. Come, Lord Jesus" (Revelation 22:20).

In this letter Paul is turning the leadership of the church over to his dear son, Timothy. Thus the Lord continues to give his church in each generation the necessary pastors and teachers to provide leadership in preserving sound doctrine and to preach his word in season and out of season with great patience and careful instruction. Pray the Lord of the harvest to send a great host of faithful laborers into his harvest throughout the world.

PERSONAL COMMENTS 4:9-18

9Do your best to come to me quickly, 10for Demas, because he loved this world, has deserted me and has gone to Thessalonica. Crescens has gone to Galatia, and Titus to Dalmatia. 11Only Luke is with me. Get Mark and bring him with you, because he is helpful to me in my ministry. 12I sent Tychicus to Ephesus. 13When you come, bring the cloak that I left with Carpus at Troas, and my scrolls, especially the parchments.

After informing Timothy that he expected soon to die a martyr's death, Paul urges him: "Do your best to come to me quickly." Paul longed once more to see his beloved son in the faith. He had expressed this already in the opening chapter (verse 4). Now he makes a direct request that Timothy come quickly. Since travel in winter would be difficult if not impossible (verse 21), Timothy should act with all due haste. In a time of crisis, what a comfort a dear friend who shares our faith can be!

The reason for urging Timothy to come quickly is that Paul is almost alone. He reports what has happened to the people who had been with him. The first person he mentions is Demas. Having been with Paul during his first imprisonment, Demas is mentioned as a fellow worker in Paul's letters to the Colossians (4:14) and to Philemon (verse 24). Now Demas has "deserted" Paul, forsaken him at this critical time and gone to Thessalonica. "Because he loved this world" is the reason Paul gives. Was it that Demas loved this life so that he was not willing to expose himself to possible persecution? Life was safer and more pleasant in Thessalonica. Or was he attracted by the allurements of the world so that he felt Christianity too restrictive? Whatever it was, he had deserted Paul and, possibly, the Christian faith. One can sense Paul's disappointment as he reports this. Pastors and fellow members feel deep disappointments when the newly confirmed soon fall away and leave the church, or when a once faithful member deserts the faith, tempted by sexual, financial or social allurements.

Two of Paul's companions had gone to other fields of labor. Crescens, mentioned only here in the New Testament, had gone to Galatia. What Paul had said about Demas deserting is not said of Crescens. We can assume that he went on another mission assignment. The same is true of Titus, whom Paul had called "my true son in our common faith" (Titus 1:4). Although Titus is not mentioned in the Book of Acts, we know from Paul's letters that he had worked especially in Corinth and on the island of Crete. Dalmatia, where Titus had now gone, was across the Adriatic from Italy, in modern Yugoslavia.

Only Luke, the doctor who was Paul's "dear friend" (Colossians 4:14), was with Paul. Luke is the author of the third Gospel and of the Book of Acts. In the latter he often writes in the first person plural, "we" or "us," indicating he was Paul's frequent companion (Acts 16:10-17; 20:5-21:18; 27; 28). What a "dear friend" he was, staying with Paul during his first imprisonment, and his sole companion as he now faced martyrdom! He was one of those friends "who sticks closer than a brother" (Proverbs 18:24).

Paul asks Timothy to bring Mark along. We are pleased to read what Paul says about Mark, for he had deserted Paul and Barnabas at Perga on their first missionary journey (Acts 13:13 "John" = John Mark, also called just Mark). When they were to begin their second journey, Barnabas wanted to take his cousin, John Mark (Colossians 4:10), along again. Paul objected, and "they had such a sharp disagreement that they parted company" (Acts 15:39). Thus Mark had been the cause for the breakup of the first mission team. Now Paul wants Mark to come to Rome "because he is helpful to me in my ministry." Mark's early discouragement did not prevent his becoming a trusted, capable servant of the Lord. And Paul did not allow his early disappointment and adverse judgment of Mark to prejudice him against Mark so that he never again trusted him. A young pastor should not allow early discouragements to cripple his entire future ministry, and older pastors should not form a permanent adverse judgment of a young pastor because of some early failure. Pastors and teachers, too, need to grow and mature in their faith through God's word and need the encouragement of older colleagues and fellow Christians.

Paul "sent" Tychicus to Ephesus, quite likely to deliver the present letter. He had similarly used this "dear brother, a faithful minister and fellow servant in the Lord" (Colossians 4:7; Ephesians 6:21), to deliver letters to the Ephesians and Colossians, and encourage them by bringing personal news from Paul during his first imprisonment in Rome.

It appears even more likely that Paul sent Tychicus to Ephesus to replace Timothy so he could follow Paul's urgent invitation to come to Rome. He is still writing of Timothy's coming, for he immediately follows with this request: "When you come, bring the cloak that I left with Carpus at Troas, and my scrolls, especially the parchments." This is a seemingly unimportant personal request that adds little to the importance and message of the letter. Nevertheless, it shows the letter's authenticity, for a forger would not have thought of including what seems a minor personal matter.

From this request we conclude that Paul must have been at Troas shortly before this and left his cloak with Carpus, a man otherwise unknown to us. The cloak was a heavy, warm capelike garment to protect against cold and rain. Looking ahead to winter in a cold, dank dungeon, Paul made this request.

In his loneliness, Paul yearned for his library, his "scrolls, especially the parchments." Parchment, made of animal skins, was durable but expensive. More common was the paper made from the papyrus plant. Books were in the form of scrolls. Paul gives no indication about what was written in those books. As a well-educated man he no doubt had studied many writings, but the Old Testament Scriptures were of prime importance. Perhaps these were the parchments he especially wanted. What could be of greater comfort to him in his loneliness than the Scriptures, which equip a man of God for every good work? In our loneliness, Scripture assures us of God's presence, for there he speaks to us. We will seek times when we can be alone with God as we read the Holy Scriptures and meditate on God's message.

[14]Alexander the metalworker did me a great deal of harm. The Lord will repay him for what he has done. [15]You too should be on your guard against him, because he strongly opposed our message.

Who was this Alexander? He does not appear to be the same as the Alexander mentioned in Acts 19:33 or the one mentioned by Paul in 1 Timothy 1:20. Neither of these is called a "metalworker." Alexander was a common name. Paul, it would seem, adds the designation "metalworker" to distinguish him from other Alexanders. Since Paul has just been urging Timothy to come to Rome, it is possible that it was there that Alexander had done Paul "a great deal of harm," and Timothy should be on his guard against him when he comes.

How had Alexander harmed Paul? And when? Why should Timothy be on his guard? "Because he strongly opposed our message," literally, "our words." Paul is about to speak of his trial. Was it there that Alexander harmed Paul, by witnessing against him and opposing what he said? We do not know, but this is a possible interpretation. Now, when Timothy and Mark come, they must guard against Alexander's damaging testimony that is also damaging to the entire cause of the gospel.

How does Paul react to the harm Alexander did to him? He is confident that "the Lord will repay him for what he has done." This does not mean that he did not speak up in his own defense against Alexander and warn against him, but he seeks no personal retribution. God will see that justice is done. Paul knew the words of David in the psalm: "Surely you [the Lord] will reward each person according to what he has done" (Psalm 62:12). To the Romans Paul had written: "Do not repay evil for evil. . . . Do not take revenge, my friends, but leave room for God's wrath, for it is written: 'It is mine to avenge; I will repay,' says the Lord" (Romans 12:17,19). Paul practiced what he taught. The pastor, or any Christian, who tries to harm or "get even with" those who harm him is taking matters into his own hands. He is acting contrary to the gospel and usurping God's role.

16At my first defense, no one came to my support, but everyone deserted me. May it not be held against them. 17But the Lord stood at my side and gave me strength, so that through me the message might be fully proclaimed and all the Gentiles might hear it. And I was delivered from the lion's mouth. 18The Lord will rescue me from every evil attack and will bring me

**safely to his heavenly kingdom. To him be glory for ever and
ever. Amen.**

"At my first defense" hardly refers back to Paul's first imprisonment and his defense at that time. Timothy was completely acquainted with it and Paul's subsequent acquittal.
Paul is informing Timothy as to what happened only recently
at his first hearing, when he was brought to trial and given an
opportunity for defense.

"No one came to my support, but everyone deserted me."
Whom is Paul speaking about? Does this again refer to
Demas' desertion? Were Crescens and Titus still in Rome
and failed to speak up for Paul? Should Luke, who was with
Paul, have spoken up? Or is he rather thinking of other
Christians or even Roman citizens, people of influence, who
knew Paul and might have stepped forward in his defense?
We do not know the answer. We know only that Paul was on
his own, "deserted" by everyone else. Nevertheless, in the
spirit of Christ (Luke 23:34) and of Stephen (Acts 7:60) he
says: "May it not be held against them."

Although Paul was on his own, he was not alone. "But the
Lord stood at my side and gave me strength." At the time of
his conversion the Lord said of Paul: "This man is my chosen
instrument to carry my name before the Gentiles and their
kings and before the people of Israel. I will show him how
much he must suffer for my name" (Acts 9:15,16). Paul
knew what to expect in the Lord's service, but he also knew
the Lord would be with him. Jesus promised his disciples:
"But when they arrest you, do not worry about what to say or
how to say it. At that time you will be given what to say, for
it will not be you speaking, but the Spirit of your Father
speaking through you" (Matthew 10:19,20). No, Paul was
not alone. A pastor is never alone, a Christian is never alone,

even in the most trying and difficult situations. God gives strength, and promises to put words into our mouths, the words he wants us to speak. That was Paul's experience.

"So that through me the message might be fully proclaimed and all the Gentiles might hear it" — thus also at his trial in making his defense, Paul was given strength to give testimony to Christ before the assembled Gentiles. Paul was ever conscious of his responsibility to the Gentiles. He wrote to the Romans: "I am obligated both to Greeks and to non-Greeks, both to the wise and the foolish. That is why I am so eager to preach the gospel also to you who are at Rome" (1:14,15). From Rome he hoped to go on to Spain. Tradition has it that he did fulfill this expectation. Now he realized that the "time had come for his departure." Once more at his trial he was given the opportunity to bring the "message" to the Gentiles. The Lord gave him strength. So he completed his assignment, even as he stood trial for his life before a Roman tribunal. The Gentile world had heard him proclaim the message fully wherever he went.

The outcome of this first hearing was that "I was delivered from the lion's mouth." Is Paul thinking of Satan, whom Peter compares to a roaring lion (1 Peter 5:8)? This is not likely. Is he saying that he was spared from being thrown to the lions, as were many Christians in the persecutions? This too is unlikely, since as a Roman citizen he would be exempt from such punishment. Even though he fully expected martyrdom as the result of his imprisonment, at this hearing he still was spared. "The lion's mouth" was his impending martyrdom. Paul recognized every day the Lord granted him as another day of grace in the Lord's service.

He looks ahead with confidence. Whatever evil he has to suffer at the hands of Rome will not destroy him. The Lord is with him, will rescue him and will bring him "safely to his heavenly kingdom." Martyrdom will lead to eternal glory. The Lord has taught us to pray, "But deliver us from evil." Luther's explanation in the *Small Catechism* is a good exposition also of Paul's words here: "We pray in this petition that our Father in heaven would deliver us from every evil that threatens body and soul, property and reputation, and finally when our last hour comes, grant us a blessed end and graciously take us from this world of sorrow to himself in heaven."

As Paul thinks of his glorious deliverance and being forever with the Lord, his heart shouts out these words of praise: "To him be glory for ever and ever. Amen" — "Yes, so shall it be." May that be the joyful response of every Christian as he confidently awaits the Lord's eternal deliverance.

CLOSING GREETINGS

Verse 18 is a fitting ending to the letter proper. Only a few greetings and comments follow.

¹⁹Greet Priscilla and Aquila and the household of Onesiphorus. ²⁰Erastus stayed in Corinth, and I left Trophimus sick in Miletus. ²¹Do your best to get here before winter. Eubulus greets you, and so do Pudens, Linus, Claudia and all the brothers.

Priscilla and Aquila were dear friends of Paul. He first met them at Corinth on his second missionary journey. Aquila, a native of Pontus, had lived in Rome but left when Emperor Claudius ordered all Jews to leave (Acts 18:1-3). Like Paul they were tentmakers, and he stayed and worked with them. They became Christians. Later they lived at Ephesus, where they "invited" Apollos "to their home and explained to him the way of God more adequately" (Acts 18:19,26). Thus they were very knowledgeable laymen. When Paul wrote his letter to the Romans, they were again in Rome, and Paul extends special greetings to them, noting that they risked their lives for him (Romans 16:3,4). Had they again left Rome when the Neronian persecutions began? Whatever the answer is, they were again at Ephesus and Paul sends greetings to them.

Paul extends special greetings also to "the household of Onesiphorus." Early in this letter Paul had spoken about him, his kindness at Rome and helpfulness in Ephesus (1:16-18). Apparently Onesiphorus himself was not at Ephesus since

171

the greetings are not extended to him personally. If he were still at Rome, we could expect Paul to mention him with those who send greetings to Timothy. Where was Onesiphorus? Had he perhaps died? Had he been martyred? We do not know. Perhaps Timothy knew. At least Paul saw no need to tell him.

Paul did, however, inform Timothy as to where Erastus and Trophimus were. It seems that Timothy might wonder why they weren't with Paul in Rome. Paul explains, "Erastus stayed in Corinth, and I left Trophimus sick in Miletus." From this we conclude that Paul had been at both of these places before his present imprisonment. Who was Erastus? An Erastus is mentioned together with Timothy as two helpers whom Paul sent from Ephesus to Macedonia (Acts 19:22). The name of Erastus also appears among those who send greetings to the Christians in Rome (Romans 16:23). He is the city's (Corinth?) director of public works. There is a question whether these are the same person. If not, it seems more likely the former is the one Paul here refers to. We assume that Erastus stayed in Corinth because his services were needed.

Trophimus is easier to identify. From Acts 20:4 and 21:29 we learn that he was "from the province of Asia," an Ephesian, who accompanied Paul to Jerusalem after his third missionary journey. Illness forced him to stay at Miletus.

Paul urgently desired the presence of Timothy. Again he reminds him to come before winter would delay his journey. But in view of what Paul had written, is he also implying that he may "depart" before the winter was over?

When Paul had said that only Luke was with him at Rome, this referred only to his co-workers. He now extends greetings from Eubulus, Pudens, Linus, Claudia and all the brothers. None of the four is mentioned elsewhere in the New

Testament. They, of course, were known to Timothy. The Lord still had his faithful few in Rome in spite of the persecutions.

22The Lord be with your spirit. Grace be with you.

These are the last words we have from the pen of Paul. What more could he wish for Timothy than the abiding presence of his Lord? What more could he wish for all who read his letter, and that includes us, than grace that spells salvation?

TITUS
INTRODUCTION

According to the listing of the pastoral letters in the New Testament, the letter to Titus is the third. It was written, however, about the same time as Paul's first letter to Timothy, possibly from Philippi in the fall of A.D. 63. For a fuller description of the historical setting of Titus and the two letters to Timothy, read again the introduction to the pastoral letters on pages 1-5, especially the section entitled "Historical Setting."

Titus, the recipient of this letter, is not mentioned in the Book of Acts, but only in Paul's letters. Besides addressing this letter to Titus, Paul refers to him in Galatians, 2 Corinthians and 2 Timothy.

Since Paul calls Titus "my true son in our common faith" (Titus 1:4), he no doubt was one of Paul's converts. He may have been from Antioch, where Paul had worked for an entire year before his missionary journeys (Acts 11:26). We find Titus there when Paul and Barnabas "were appointed, along with some other believers, to go up to Jerusalem to see the apostles and elders" about the necessity of circumcision for salvation (Acts 15:2). Paul mentions Titus as someone he had taken along as a test case and reports that "not even Titus, who was with me, was compelled to be circumcised, even though he was a Greek" (Galatians 2:1,3).

Later Paul found Titus to be a valuable and trusted associate whom he sent to Corinth to settle the problems that had arisen in this congregation. Paul expected him to report back at Troas (2 Corinthians 2:12,13). When Paul did not find him there, Paul went on to Macedonia, where he received a favorable report from Titus. His mission to Corinth had been successful (2 Corinthians 7:6,7,13,14). After reporting to Paul, Titus returned to Corinth to provide needed encouragement to continue gathering the collection for the poor in Jerusalem (2 Corinthians 8:6,16,17; 12:18). In all his Corinthian assignments Titus proved to be an evangelical, trusted and respected "troubleshooter."

After Paul's release from his first imprisonment, he may have met Titus when he came to the island of Crete. Paul left Titus there to complete the organizing of the church (Titus 1:5). This was not an easy assignment because of troublemakers who needed correction (Titus 1:10-16). Paul promised to send a replacement to Crete so that Titus might join him again at Nicopolis where Paul intended to spend the winter (Titus 3:12).

Finally, Titus must have been with Paul in Rome during a part of his second imprisonment, for Paul sent him from Rome to Dalmatia (2 Timothy 4:10). We know nothing more about this assignment.

Titus no doubt was younger than Paul but very likely older than Timothy. He did not need the kind of encouragement that Paul gave his younger "son" Timothy. The advice Paul gave Titus for his work on the island of Crete continues to be a blessing to the church and its pastors as they read, study and apply his inspired words to themselves and the church of all times.

Outline of Titus

Opening Greeting 1:1-4

I. Titus' Assignment in Crete 1:5-16
   A. Complete What Still Needs to Be Done 1:5

OPENING GREETING
TITUS 1:1-4

1 **Paul, a servant of God and an apostle of Jesus Christ for the faith of God's elect and the knowledge of the truth that leads to godliness—²a faith and knowledge resting on the hope of eternal life, which God, who does not lie, promised before the beginning of time, ³and at his appointed season he brought his word to light through the preaching entrusted to me by the command of God our Savior.**

Obviously Paul is not writing this letter only for Titus, for him to read and file away. If it were only for Titus, the lengthy assertion concerning himself and his ministry would not be necessary. For the people whom Titus was serving in Crete, however, where Paul had been only a short time, it was important to be reminded that the writer was "a servant of God and an apostle of Jesus Christ."

Paul is "a servant of God," literally a slave, one who takes orders from none other than God. Paul's will is subject to God's will. He preached and wrote what God wanted preached and written. This is important to remember when reading Paul's letter.

In addition, Paul calls himself an "apostle of Jesus Christ," one who was "sent out" by Jesus himself. On the way to Damascus, Jesus confronted him and sent him into the city where he was met by Ananias to whom God had revealed that "this man is my chosen instrument to carry my name before the Gentiles and their kings and before the people of

Israel" (Acts 9:15). Jesus, the Head of the church, had commissioned Paul even as he had sent the "twelve."

Paul's commission was "for the faith of God's elect and the knowledge of the truth that leads to godliness." He was "sent to help God's chosen people to believe and to know the truth which promotes godliness" (*GWN*). Faith, knowledge of the truth and godliness are closely interrelated. "How . . . can they believe in one of whom they have not heard?" (Romans 10:14) "Faith by itself, if it is not accompanied by action, is dead" (James 2:17). Godliness is faith in action.

The Christian's entire faith and life of piety, however, are built on hope, the very special "hope of eternal life." The unbeliever's hopes extend only to this life. He hopes for a life of ease, for riches, for honor, for a pleasant retirement. But, "if only for this life we have hope in Christ, we are to be pitied more than all men" (1 Corinthians 15:19). Christ did not redeem us for a longer and better life in a world of sin. There has to be more to life than what we experience in the here and now. There is: eternal life, the Christian's hope.

This hope is not a pipe dream. It has been promised by "God, who does not lie." Satan is the father of lies and makes lying promises. God's promises are true, sure and certain. With the passing of time they are not terminated but fulfilled. They were made "before the beginning of time," when God already determined in his heart to bring his chosen ones to a blessed eternity through his beloved Son as Savior.

In fulfilling his promises God uses his own time schedule. "When the time had fully come, God sent his Son" (Galatians 4:4). God also determines by whom the message of his Son is to be preached. "At his appointed season he brought his word to light through the preaching entrusted to me by the command of God our Savior." Paul was a chosen servant of God and an apostle, entrusted with a message and functioning under a divine command. No one ever preached God's word more widely and more clearly than the Apostle Paul. The people of Crete were to know that what Paul had preached among them, what Titus his true son in the faith was preaching, and what they read in this letter was indeed the word of God, a revelation of God's promises and fulfillment in Christ, proclaimed by God's authorized messenger.

We still are the favored recipients of the preaching that God enjoined upon Paul. Through it God continues to bring to light his word, the gospel of Christ. God planned it that way. The whole of Scripture becomes clearer as a result of the revelation God granted through the preaching of this inspired apostle. No wonder that the letters to the Romans and to the Galatians and all of Paul's letters were favorites of Luther. Whoever does not study the writings of the apostle Paul will deprive himself of the clearest revelation in Scripture of salvation by grace through faith in the Lord Jesus Christ. Pastors, teachers, Christians, take and read what God brought to light at his appointed season through his servant Paul!

⁴To Titus, my true son in our common faith:

Grace and peace from God the Father and Christ Jesus our Savior.

After the lengthy paragraph establishing his divinely given mandate, Paul addresses Titus, the recipient of this letter. "My true son in our common faith" reminds us of the way he addressed Timothy (1 Timothy 1:2). Like Timothy, Titus was one of Paul's converts. Unlike Timothy, who had a Jewish mother, Titus was a Gentile.

Paul wishes Titus the grace and peace that God alone can give. While he usually refers to Christ Jesus as our Lord, he here calls him "our Savior." In the previous verse he had referred to God as "our Savior." Yes, the entire Trinity is "our Savior." How comforting to know that God, Father, Son and Holy Spirit, is indeed and can be called "our Savior!"

TITUS' ASSIGNMENT IN CRETE
TITUS 1:5-16

Complete What Still Needs to Be Done

⁵The reason I left you in Crete was that you might straighten out what was left unfinished and appoint elders in every town, as I directed you.

The ship that took Paul, the prisoner, to Rome had stopped briefly on the island of Crete, in the Mediterranean Sea south of Greece (Acts 27:7,8). After his release, Paul appears to have stopped there on his way to Ephesus and to have done some mission work together with Titus. Cretans already are mentioned among those present in Jerusalem at the first Pentecost (Acts 2:11). By the time Paul left Crete to continue to Ephesus and Philippi, groups of Christians could be found in every town on this island.

"Unfinished" work waited to be done, however, especially that of appointing elders in the various towns. Before Paul left, he told Titus to take care of these matters. Now he gives Titus instructions also in writing. He expects soon to send another man, either Artemas or Tychicus (3:12), to replace Titus so that he can join Paul at Nicopolis before winter.

Paul gives no detailed instructions on how the churches are to be organized. Most important is that they have qualified elders, or pastors. How these were appointed we are not told. It would be wrong to assume that Titus made these appointments without consulting the congregations. It seems likely that he proceeded much as the congregation in Jerusalem did when they needed deacons (Acts 6:2-6), through some form of election. God nowhere gives specific commands how our congregations are to call their pastors and teachers. Rather than showing concern for the procedure, Paul stresses the qualifications of the appointees.

Qualifications of Elders

⁶An elder must be blameless, the husband of but one wife, a man whose children believe and are not open to the charge of being wild and disobedient. ⁷Since an overseer is entrusted with God's work, he must be blameless — not overbearing, not quick-tempered, not given to drunkenness, not violent, not pursuing dishonest gain. ⁸Rather he must be hospitable, one who loves what is good, who is self-controlled, upright, holy and disciplined. ⁹He must hold firmly to the trustworthy message as it has been taught, so that he can encourage others by sound doctrine and refute those who oppose it.

In appointing elders in every town, Titus and the congregations were to look for men with the right qualifications. What were these qualifications? He had written them also to Timothy, where he had included the qualifications of deacons and their wives (1 Timothy 3:2-12). As he writes to Titus, he mentions only elders or overseers. These new congregations did not require all the offices already needed in the older Ephesus congregation. Nevertheless, the two lists are very similar. The qualifications for elders or pastors do not change from place to place or from time to time. They still apply today. The pastor's prayer will ever be: Lord, help me live up to them to your glory!

Paul begins with "blameless," a broad, general qualification (cf. 1 Timothy 3:2,10). "He should be the kind of person who cannot be accused openly and publicly" (Luther). His marital life should be above reproach, "the husband of but one wife" (cf. 1 Timothy 3:2,12). His children should be such who "believe and are not open to the charge of being wild and disobedient" (cf. 1 Timothy 3:4,5). Here Paul says that also the elder's children are to be "believers," a point not made in writing to Timothy. This may reflect conditions in the young churches that were being organized in Crete. Men whose families were still pagan and who showed that they could not properly carry out Christian discipline in the home should not be chosen to lead a congregation as elders.

As Paul in verse 7 continues to list the qualifications, he uses the term "overseer," also translated "bishop" (*KJV*). "Elder" stressed the Christian maturity, "overseer" the ruling, leadership function of someone "entrusted with God's work." The word can be translated "manager" or "steward." Never should a pastor forget that he has been entrusted to manage God's work. That is why he needs to be "blameless." Everything he does reflects on our gracious God and affects God's work.

After referring again to this general qualification, Paul elaborates further with five negatives: "not overbearing," not self-pleasing or arrogant. "This refers to that stern and haughty attitude which looks at itself in the mirror and despises others" (Luther). The overseer must be "not quick-tempered," prone to anger, often linked with arrogance; "not given to drunkenness" (cf. 1 Timothy 3:3); "not violent" (cf. 1 Timothy 3:3), that is, not contentious and quarrelsome; "not pursuing dishonest gain" (cf. 1 Timothy 3:8), thus "not a lover of money" (cf. 1 Timothy 3:3).

Now follow positive qualifications: "hospitable" (cf. 1 Timothy 3:2); "loves what is good." "Let him be prepared to advance such causes as piety, sacred letters, peace, harmony, and friendship among neighbors. . . . Let him be zealous to help good persons and good issues" (Luther). He must be "self-controlled" (cf. 1 Timothy 3:2), not impulsive but sober-minded; "upright," just and fair in dealing with others; "holy," pious in his personal conduct; "disciplined," keeping control of his sensual appetites.

Paul concludes with what must be considered the most important qualification. All other items mentioned will not qualify a man to be a pastor (elder, overseer) if this final one is missing. "He must hold firmly to the trustworthy message as it has been taught." Overseers, pastors, must be sure of their doctrine, of the message they proclaim. They can be sure when they hold firmly to the message or word "as it has been taught," that is, by Paul and his associate Titus. Paul is not directing all future pastors simply to hold firmly to everything their former teachers may have taught them. It is not enough to be able to say that this is what Luther taught, or our pastor, or a respected professor. Everything they taught us that is based on the word of Christ and his chosen, inspired apostles is "trustworthy." We too must hold to it firmly, always.

The reason this qualification is essential for an elder is "so that he can encourage others by sound doctrine and refute those who oppose it." There is a positive and a negative aspect to a pastor's ministry. Only sound, or healthy, doctrine can "encourage," that is, produce or strengthen faith, comfort, guide, inspire, nourish. Any substitute is giving husks instead of the kernel.

The pastor also needs to defend the flock against those who oppose sound doctrine. Because of the many false religions and erroneous teachings threatening the flock, the pastor needs a firm grip on the "trustworthy message." He must be well equipped for this negative aspect of his ministry, that of "convincing the gainsayers" (KJV). Crete was not lacking in them, as Paul now shows. No age in the church's history is without them. The church dare never fail to recognize the importance of this final qualification.

Problems in Crete

10For there are many rebellious people, mere talkers and deceivers, especially those of the circumcision group. 11They must be silenced, because they are ruining whole households by teaching things they ought not to teach — and that for the sake of dishonest gain. 12Even one of their own prophets has said, "Cretans are always liars, evil brutes, lazy gluttons." 13This testimony is true. Therefore, rebuke them sharply, so that they will be sound in the faith 14and will pay no attention to Jewish myths or to the commands of those who reject the truth. 15To the pure, all things are pure, but to those who are corrupted and do not believe, nothing is pure. In fact, both their minds and consciences are corrupted. 16They claim to know God, but by their actions they deny him. They are detestable, disobedient and unfit for doing anything good.

The "overseers" Titus was to appoint in Crete were to refute those who oppose sound doctrine. This was not only a warning against false teachers in general. Paul was referring to specific people in Crete and now describes them. That is not to say that the description does not fit those who oppose sound doctrine in every age and place.

Paul calls them "rebellious people," not willing to be subject to a higher authority like that of Scripture or Paul, the apostle of God. Today, a growing number of so-called Christian teachers and leaders will not recognize Scripture as an infallible authority. They place their own reason and ideas above Scripture and refuse to follow its clear teaching.

They are "mere talkers and deceivers." They talk a lot but don't say anything. Theirs is "meaningless talk" (1 Timothy

1:6). With empty talk they deceive people. They want to convince their hearers that they possess a higher and more profound understanding of Christianity and the Scriptures. Actually they are destroying it.

There were many such opponents in Crete, but the worst were "those of the circumcision group." These were Jews who seemingly had converted to Christianity but insisted on the need for circumcision and certain Old Testament ceremonial laws. They had been dealt with at the council in Jerusalem (Acts 15). Paul opposed them in his letter to the Galatians: "Mark my words! I, Paul, tell you that if you let yourselves be circumcised, Christ will be of no value to you at all" (Galatians 5:2). This was a serious matter. "They must be silenced," Paul writes to Titus. How? By means of sound doctrine.

Their deceptive, empty talk was dangerous and had had damaging results. "They are ruining whole households (literally houses) by teaching things they ought not to teach." Complete families were being mislead and brought to spiritual ruin. The word "household" goes even beyond the actual family members to servants and any others in some way connected with the family. Perhaps it even included people who would meet in a particular house as a small "house" church.

Like the false teachers against whom Paul warns Timothy "who think that godliness is a means to financial gain" (1 Timothy 6:5), these errorists were out to make "dishonest gain." They were motivated by love for money rather than love for souls. What they were doing was deceptive and dishonest and destructive of Christianity.

This reminds Paul, a man of considerable education, of a quotation from a prominent poet of Crete (Epimenides, writing in the 6th century B.C.). Paul calls him "one of their own prophets." He was not, of course, a prophet of God, but one who was considered among his people as a spokesman of the gods. In this quotation he spoke out regarding the vices and evils of his people: "Cretans are always liars, evil brutes, lazy gluttons."

This was not an "outsider" making a racist statement. This was a Cretan speaking the truth about his own people. They had this reputation and deserved it. "This testimony is true," was also God's judgment, spoken through the inspired apostle. Sometimes there are special vices, particular sins, that are prominent in a given society. The city of Corinth had a reputation for immorality, and Sodom gave its name, sodomy, to unnatural sexual practices. Titus and the "overseers" needed to understand the special problems they faced in doing their work among the Cretans. We must know the opponent if we are effectively to oppose him.

The people of Crete were not beyond the reach of the gospel, but it was necessary to "rebuke them sharply." Clear, plain language, spoken sincerely and earnestly, was needed in opposing the deceiving teachers and their deceived followers. Sin must be called sin, and error must be shown for what it is and rigorously corrected.

The goal in correcting people's sins is not academic or simply improved morals. The stern rebuke has the purpose "that they will be sound in the faith." Sound faith requires sound doctrine. This means that they "pay no attention to Jewish myths or to the commands of those who reject the truth."

Paul gave a warning against "Jewish myths" also to Timothy when Paul urged him to command certain men not to devote themselves to "myths and endless genealogies" (1 Timothy 1:4). The many Jewish speculations that were added to the Old Testament destroyed the saving Gospel with its free salvation in Christ. The higher knowledge they claimed for their speculations reminds us of later gnosticism (from "*gnosis*" which means knowledge) with its way to salvation through the unique knowledge its adherents claimed to have.

These people who rejected the truth sought to enslave others by the commands they imposed on them. To Timothy he wrote about the "hypocritical liars" who "forbid people to marry and order them to abstain from certain foods" (1 Timothy 4:2,3). That Paul may be referring to similar commands made by the Cretan deceivers can be concluded from what follows.

"To the pure, all things are pure, but to those who are corrupted and do not believe, nothing is pure." Jesus had said: "What goes into a man's mouth does not make him 'unclean,' but what comes out of his mouth, that is what makes him 'unclean'" (Matthew 15:11). The Jews were much concerned not to contaminate themselves with anything unclean. "Do not handle! Do not taste! Do not touch!" Paul said of "such regulations" that they "indeed have an appearance of wisdom, with their self-imposed worship, their false humility and their harsh treatment of the body, but they lack any value in restraining sensual indulgence" (Colossians 2:23). The truth is that "everything God created is good, and nothing is to be rejected if it is received with thanksgiving" (1 Timothy 4:4). "To the pure, all things are pure."

On the other hand, when "both their minds and consciences are corrupted," when there is no faith in the purifying power of Christ Jesus, "nothing is pure." The person with a corrupted mind makes whatever he touches impure and whoever has a corrupted conscience cannot serve God in moral purity. "Without faith it is impossible to please God" (Hebrews 11:6).

Paul has a serious indictment against these deceitful teachers in Crete. "They claim to know God, but by their actions they deny him. They are detestable, disobedient and unfit for doing anything good." They spoke about God and spoke with much authority, as though they knew God better than anyone else. Their actions, however, were a denial of what they confessed with their mouths. They were hypocritical deceivers. Nothing they did was good in the eyes of God, who is the final judge of everything. "A bad tree cannot bear good fruit" (Matthew 7:18).

"Rebellious," "mere talkers and deceivers," "detestable, disobedient and unfit for doing anything good" — that is Paul's description of the false teachers in Crete whom Titus must oppose and rebuke sharply. That description fits all false teachers. They may indeed "claim to know God," but, eventually, "by their actions they deny him." "By their fruit you will recognize them" (Matthew 7:16) was our Savior's advice.

In view of what Paul had said of the Cretans, a warning is in place here. Pastors, yes, we all, must guard against stereotyping every member of a certain race or nationality. We must guard against letting prejudices develop which will hinder our gospel work. It may be helpful to recognize that certain characteristics are present in certain cultures or races or nationalities. Paul recognized that "Jews demand miraculous signs and Greeks look for wisdom" (1 Corinthians 1:22). Thus he realized that preaching Christ crucified was "a stumbling block to Jews and foolishness to Gentiles" (verse 23). This did not hinder his preaching the crucified Christ to both, and with success. We must ever realize that we are all sinners, proclaiming Christ crucified to people who are sinners. The same Christ is the only saving means for us all. This is the power and wisdom of God that wins victories for God among all races and nations and cultures throughout the world.

189

Jesus Teaching the People by the Seaside

TITUS MUST TEACH SOUND DOCTRINE
TITUS 2:1-15

2 **You must teach what is in accord with sound doctrine.**

Paul had finished describing the false teachers whom Titus is confronting in Crete, calling them "detestable, disobedient and unfit for doing anything good." Now he addresses Titus, "But as for you . . . " (*GWN*). The original makes this a strong contrast between Titus and the false teachers. Titus must teach "in accord with sound doctrine," a refrain that echoes repeatedly throughout the pastoral epistles (1:9; 1 Timothy 1:10). This first verse introduces the second chapter.

In this chapter Paul instructs Titus on what he by contrast must teach the various groups within the congregations, the older men, the older women, the younger women, the younger men and the slaves. They must learn how they are to live and conduct themselves as believing children of God. Paul, however, not only gives instruction but also points to the power source for such living, the motivating influence of the "grace of God that brings salvation" which "has appeared to all men" (2:11).

To the Older Men

2Teach the older men to be temperate, worthy of respect, self-controlled, and sound in faith, in love and in endurance.

The "older men" whom Titus is to teach are not the same as the "elders" who were elected to a position of responsibility in the congregation. About them Paul had written in chapter 1. Here he has in mind the older men of the congregation who because of their age and maturity were looked to for leadership and exemplary Christian behavior. To a great extent the attitudes and characteristics they are to be taught are the same as those mentioned by Paul already in the first chapter as well as in his first letter to Timothy concerning elders, deacons and deaconesses.

The "older men" are to learn to be "temperate," literally, "sober, abstaining from wine" (cf. 1:7; 1 Timothy 3:2), but refers also to mental sobriety. They are to be "worthy of respect," displaying the dignity that should come with maturity. He should "not behave as though he wanted to be an adolescent" (Luther, cf. 1 Timothy 3:8). Older men ought to be "self-controlled," sensible, of sound mind (cf. 1:8; 1 Timothy 3:2). "The old men ought to be the balance-wheel of every congregation" (Lenski). Finally, they must learn to be "sound," that is, healthy, "in faith, in love and in endurance." Spiritual health is found where there is a faith that trusts in God and his revealed truth, where love reaches out with the selflessness that responds to and is inspired by God's love for a sinful world, where patience is joined to love which endures all things, knowing that a loving God lets all things work for our good.

Blessed is the congregation that has "older men" who fit this description. Happy is the pastor who can rely on such mature, sound leadership on the part of seasoned, sensible, sober "older men." This is a blessing God grants as a pastor faithfully teaches "sound doctrine."

To the Older Women

3Likewise, teach the older women to be reverent in the way they live, not to be slanderers or addicted to much wine, but to

teach what is good. ⁴Then they can train the younger women to love their husbands and children, ⁵to be self-controlled and pure, to be busy at home, to be kind, and to be subject to their husbands, so that no one will malign the word of God.

Like the older men, the older women are to be taught to fill an important place in the congregation. First, in the "way they live," they are to be "reverent," that is, conduct themselves in a way that is fitting for holy persons or believers. This may correspond to the dignity that is expected of the older men. The older women are "not to be slanderers" (cf. 1 Timothy 3:11), or to be yielding to the temptation to spread "idle gossip," a temptation for "older women" no less than for "younger widows" (1 Timothy 5:13).

Like the older men, the older women are warned against becoming "addicted to much wine." The older women may attempt to overcome the boredom of idleness and loneliness with slanderous gossip and too much wine. That is not a "way of life" befitting godliness. The older women can serve in a way that is indeed useful and beneficial to their fellow Christians. They should "teach what is good." In the succeeding verses Paul instructs Titus regarding a specific teaching role of older women that is of great importance for the future of the church's families.

The younger women need training as wives and mothers. Who can do that better than the older women? Titus is to enlist them, and Paul here gives him the specifics of this training. The older women can train the younger women by word and example to love their husbands and children. Yes, love requires training. It isn't just an emotional feeling that happens and is beyond a person's control, something especially younger people fall into. It doesn't selfishly look for personal fulfillment. Love gives, sacrifices, acts—something the older women may have learned from experience. Christ's love is the perfect example and source. First Corinthians 13 gives the perfect description. Where there is training in such love, the thought of divorce does not arise, and the children that God gives will not be unwanted. This is a basic, important ingredient of family life training.

"Self-controlled," or "sensible," is mentioned here as with each age group. In human relations, as people live together in a family, all need to practice this virtue.

They are to be "pure," or "chaste." The sixth commandment with its prohibition against adultery protects the family. While younger women are to be "pure," the same applies to their spouses. "Cheating" by either spouse destroys the unity of the family. Christians must flee the temptations with which a sexually free society entices them. Let no one forget the deadly effects of impurity. It destroys marriages. It kills faith.

The younger women are to be trained "to be busy at home." To be a "homemaker" or "housewife" is a noble task. In the home the wife and mother can make the greatest contribution toward a healthy family life. A society that places a higher value on the paycheck a wife brings to the family than on what she does for her family at home will experience the breakdown of family life. The woman's role in the family is not determined by society but by the Lord who created man and woman and established the family. Proverbs 31:10-31 is an inspired description of a "wife of noble character." It does not rule out her functioning as a "breadwinner," but does stress her place as a "homemaker."

The younger women should be trained to be "kind, and to be subject to their husbands." A woman who is "kind," who wants to do what is "good," will not find it difficult to follow God's will "to be subject to her husband." Much has had to be written to show that this is not a demeaning submission that makes her any less a beloved child of God than her husband. She will recognize her position in marriage as the role her loving Savior has given her (cf. Ephesians 5:22; Colossians 3:18; 1 Peter 3:1), one that in a special way contributes to the unity and well-being of the family.

The younger women, thus trained, can indeed make a significant contribution, "so that no one will malign the word of God." The ungodly, pagan world looks for every opportunity to speak evil of God's word. Through our failure to live according to his word we must not give maligners opportunity to malign. No Christian will want to do anything that brings harm to the gospel and hinders its work in the hearts of sinners. The loving, self-controlled, kind, submissive conduct of wives can do its part in bringing unbelieving husbands into God's fold (1 Peter 3:1).

Paul assigns the training of the younger women, not directly to Titus, but to the older women. Older women with their experience and with the proper qualifications could teach the younger women about family life better than Titus, a man, perhaps approaching forty. The church can call on capable men and women who may be able to teach and counsel in special situations where they have specific experience and gifts. Paul also may not have wanted to expose Titus to the temptations present in counseling and training younger women. For the teaching of all other age groups Paul makes Titus directly responsible.

To the Young Men

⁶Similarly, encourage the young men to be self-controlled. ⁷In everything set them an example by doing what is good. In your teaching show integrity, seriousness ⁸and soundness of speech that cannot be condemned, so that those who oppose

you may be ashamed because they have nothing bad to say about us.

"Similarly encourage the young men to be self-controlled." We already noted that all age groups are admonished to be self-controlled. This is the only specific virtue that Paul mentions in regard to the young men. At an age when youthful passions press for satisfaction and fulfillment, self-control is most necessary. Above all, the young men should be urged to conduct themselves sensibly, to use reasoned judgment rather than following their youthful impulses.

With this age group Paul calls on Titus to "set them an example by doing what is good." As such he will, of course, also be an example to all the members of the congregation, whatever their age or sex. The young men especially, at a time when they are forming habits and character and looking for heroes to imitate, can look to Titus "in everything" as their model in "doing what is good."

This places a heavy responsibility on Titus. As he teaches the young men and others, he must show "integrity, seriousness and soundness of speech that cannot be condemned." It must be clear that he is a man of his word, that what he says is trustworthy. The manner in which he speaks should not be flippant, perhaps even speaking in a joking manner of things sacred, but dignified without being stiff and formal. He is to be serious about what he says. In every way his words should reflect soundness of teaching and understanding. Titus is to be a good representative of his Savior so that no one can bring accusations against him and his teaching. Opponents there will be, but the soundness of Titus' teaching and conduct should stop any attempt to speak evil about Christians.

May God grant his church many such young pastors and teachers who serve as examples to our church's youth, yes, to all its members. Not only will they inspire good Christian habits in those who follow them, but the word of God, the gospel, will be well spoken of. Other young men will be moved to follow their pastor's example also in wanting to become pastors themselves. The exemplary enthusiasm for service and love of God's word on the part of pastors and teachers will inspire other young men and women to prepare for the teaching and preaching ministries.

To the Slaves

⁹Teach slaves to be subject to their masters in everything, to try to please them, not to talk back to them, ¹⁰and not to steal from them, but to show that they can be fully trusted, so that in every way they will make the teaching about God our Savior attractive.

Slavery was part of the social structure in the Roman Empire. Thus we find Paul repeatedly giving instructions to slaves and masters (1 Timothy 6:1-2; 1 Corinthians 7:20-22; Ephesians 6:5-9; Colossians 3:22-4:1; Philemon 16). Titus is to impress on the slaves in Crete who had become Christians that their lives now must differ from those of pagan slaves.

Slaves labor under enforced obedience. Titus should teach them "to be subject to their masters in everything," thus to render willing obedience at all times, not only when they have no choice. They must be intent on trying to please their masters, and not only when their masters please them (1 Peter 2:18). They are not to talk back to their masters, demonstrating a spirit of insubordination. From Paul's description of the Cretans, we can infer that there may have been much pilfering on the part of slaves. Christian slaves will be different, not stealing from their masters. Rather, they must show that they could be "fully trusted."

Pagan masters, noting this difference in their Christian slaves, would see the wholesome effect which Christian teaching had in their slave's attitude and conduct. Thus "in every way they will make the teaching about God our Savior attractive." The slaves' position in Roman society might be a lowly one, but what a gloriously honored position it was to make the gospel attractive to their heathen masters, possibly to be instrumental in leading them to the only Savior God.

These words of Paul surely have much broader application than only to those who literally are slaves. Also in a society that rejects slavery there are those who serve in positions that require one to follow a superior's orders. Willing service, complete honesty and trustworthiness must characterize the Christian in the workplace.

In urging the various age groups to live their Christianity, Paul repeatedly shows the effect their lives as Christians have upon the word of God. As Christians we want to bring honor and not disgrace on the saving gospel. We will not want to be the cause for whatever evil is spoken against Christ and his word. May Christ be glorified in our lives, whether we are men or women, young or old!

Gospel Motivation

[11]For the grace of God that brings salvation has appeared to all men. [12]It teaches us to say "No" to ungodliness and worldly passions, and to live self-controlled, upright and godly lives in this present age, [13]while we wait for the blessed hope — the glorious appearing of our great God and Savior, Jesus Christ, [14]who gave himself for us to redeem us from all wickedness and to purify for himself a people that are his very own, eager to do what is good.

After encouraging believers of every age and station to live godly lives, Paul continues with a paragraph that begins with "for." The reason follows why Christians will want to live in a way that brings glory to God. Paul now provides the motive for Christian living. What is more, he shows us what gives Christians both the will and strength to resist sin and serve their Savior. What follows is a beautiful, heart-warming presentation of the gospel.

"For the grace of God that brings salvation has appeared to all men." The grace of God, his rich, undeserved love, was seen on this earth in the person of Jesus Christ, the incarnate Son of God. There is no question that Paul here speaks of Jesus' first appearance at his incarnation. Look at Jesus as he was born, lived, died, was raised, and you see the grace of God active for our salvation.

"Has appeared to all men" is a possible translation. Also possible, and we believe preferable according to the original, is pairing "the grace of God" with "all men." The sentence would then be rendered: "The grace of God that brings salvation to all people has appeared." This is how it is rendered in many Bible translations. In Christ, salvation has come to the world, to all people. "God so loved the world that he gave his one and only Son" (John 3:16). Only those who believe actually benefit from this salvation, but in Christ it has come for all. What a comfort for every sinner to know that he or she is included in God's saving grace revealed in Christ Jesus! What God's grace accomplished for sinners is spoken of in verse 14.

This grace of God in Christ "teaches us to say 'No' to ungodliness and worldly passions." But doesn't the law teach us to say "No"? Doesn't the fifth commandment tell us to say "No" when we are tempted to strike our neighbor? And to say "No" to drugs and whatever destroys life? Doesn't the sixth commandment tell us to say "No" to fornication and adultery? Doesn't the seventh commandment say "No" to all forms of theft and dishonesty? Certainly the law commands us to say "No" and threatens deadly consequences if we don't. Yes, the law tells me that I should say "No" to ungodliness and worldly passions. That's all it can do, however. It cannot bring about obedience, except a grudging compliance for selfish reasons.

The grace of God in Christ, the gospel, "teaches" us to say "No" by effecting a change within us, by moving us to say "No" from the heart. It not only teaches us to say "No," but also to "live self-controlled, upright and godly lives in this present age." The teaching of the grace of God in Christ is quite different from that of the law, which only tells us what is right and what is wrong. God's grace provides the reason, the strength, the will to do what pleases God. That is effective teaching.

The "present age" during which we are to live godly lives is a time of waiting. When we keep in mind what we as recipients of God's grace are waiting for, we are moved to serve God according to his will. This is a time during which "we wait for the blessed hope — the glorious appearing of our great God and Savior, Jesus Christ." We look forward to our Savior's second appearance, which will be in glory. Then all hopes bound up in him will be fully and completely realized. Our hope is for an inheritance that Peter describes as one that "can never perish, spoil or fade — kept in heaven for you" (1 Peter 1:4). What a joy when the Lord Jesus appears again in glory to fulfill all our hopes that are sure and certain in him! They are sure in him because he is "our great God and Savior."

Paul now reminds us what "our great God and Savior" did for our salvation. Read! Believe! And rejoice! He "gave himself for us to redeem us from all wickedness and to purify for himself a people that are his very own, eager to do what is good." To redeem requires a price. Jesus gave himself, "his holy precious blood and innocent suffering and death." He as our substitute paid the price for us. Redemption results in a setting free. We have been freed from "all wickedness" of which we were guilty and which condemned us. To redeem results in belonging to the one who paid the price, to be "a people that are his very own," or as Peter said it, "You are a chosen people . . . a people belonging to God" (1 Peter 2:9). "You are not your own; you were bought at a price" (1 Corinthians 6:19,20). We belong, yes, we belong to none other than to our great God and Savior, Jesus Christ. We belong because we have been redeemed by him. That makes us something special. Think about it!

Belonging to him, we now are "eager to do what is good." We have been purified by the cleansing blood of Jesus, now we will eagerly strive to become ever more pure in everything we do. Indeed, the gospel moves us to do, willingly and eagerly, what God in his law demands. The gospel that Paul has again so beautifully outlined for us is essential if we are to follow the instructions he has given to the various groups for Christian living. The gospel is the power source for all the good we as Christians do.

15These, then, are the things you should teach. Encourage and rebuke with all authority. Do not let anyone despise you.

Titus is to encourage and rebuke "with all authority." The minister of the word has a position of authority. This does not mean that a pastor is to step up in an imperious manner, demanding obedience to whatever he says. The authority he has comes from the word of God. He is not to Lord it over the flock, but he is with authority to direct it to God's infallible word. He must see to it that the authority of God's word is upheld.

Jesus in the Synagogue

Paul tells Titus: "Do not let anyone despise you," not because he should seek honor for himself, but because he is sent by God to teach his word. "Especially those whose work is preaching and teaching" are "worthy of double honor" (1 Timothy 5:17).

REMINDERS FOR DOING WHAT IS GOOD
TITUS 3:1-11

Doing What Is Good

3 **Remind the people to be subject to rulers and authorities, to be obedient, to be ready to do whatever is good, ²to slander no one, to be peaceable and considerate, and to show true humility toward all men.**

Having told Titus what he is to teach the men and women, young and old, about their conduct within the congregation, Paul tells him to remind Christians how they are to conduct themselves in the world. "Remind the people." Yes, Christians need reminders, frequent reminders to live their Christianity. How quickly we can forget!

Paul begins with the Christian's attitude and conduct toward governmental authority. We all live under some form of government. "Be subject to rulers and authorities." The Cretan Christians might think that their freedom in Christ freed them from obedience to secular rulers, particularly if they were pagan, as was true in the Roman Empire. As to the Jews, they always were loath to obey pagans, for the Jews were the people of God who had lived in a theocracy. In the Old Testament, God had given them their civil laws. Government and religion were closely bound together. Strict Jews never thought that they should be subject to pagan Rome. People of Jewish background, when they converted to Christianity, might bring along a negative attitude toward

heathen rulers. "Be subject," "be obedient," Titus is to remind them. By using two terms, "rulers and authorities,"
Paul shows that this applies to all levels and kinds of government. Christians will be loyal citizens in the local communi-
ties, in the state, in their nation (cf. 1 Timothy 2:1-3; Romans
13:1-7; 1 Peter 2:13-16). The only restriction to obedience
occurs when government commands us to act against God's
will. Our response then must be, "We must obey God rather
than men!" (Acts 5:29).

Just because I consider a particular law foolish or even un-
just does not allow me to disobey. Just because I consider a
tax excessive or unfair does not allow me to refuse to pay or
to "cheat" on my tax return. On the other hand, if a law were
to demand that after a family has two children any further
pregnancy must be terminated by abortion, a Christian would
have to disobey. The government may pass laws that permit
sinful actions, like some divorce laws. A Christian is not
forced to make use of them and will not consider following a
sinful course of action because it is legal. Few, however, are
the laws in most nations that actually compel a citizen to do
what is sinful. If there are such, a Christian, remaining obedient in all else, will not obey them.

Christians should be known as people who are "ready to
do whatever is good," who "slander no one," who do not find
pleasure in speaking evil of others, even if it is true.

They are "to be peaceable," not contentious, helping to
settle quarrels rather than cause them; "considerate," willing
to overlook weaknesses in others, gentle, kind, forbearing;
"and to show true humility toward all men." The word for
"humility" is also translated gentleness, courtesy, meekness.
All of these show a sensitivity and concern for the other person. Jesus calls himself "gentle," or "meek," as he invites the
"weary and burdened" to come to him for rest. Those who

accept his invitation find a gentle Savior. They find the perfect example of the kindness and courtesy and humility with which they will reach out to one another and to the troubled in the world.

Man's Sinful Nature

³At one time we too were foolish, disobedient, deceived and enslaved by all kinds of passions and pleasures. We lived in malice and envy, being hated and hating one another.

As in chapter two, Paul's encouragement to Christian living (sanctification) is followed by a gospel presentation that provides the motivation (verses 4-7). Before he does so, however, he reminds himself and Titus and the Christians in Crete and all of us of our "one time" corrupt, lost condition. Such a reminder helps us appreciate the gospel.

"At one time," the time before we had come to know and believe in the Lord Jesus, "we too were foolish." Not that we thought so. Unbelievers often think themselves to be very wise. Paul, before he was a Christian, thought he was wise in following the ways of the self-righteous Pharisees and, therefore, in persecuting the Christians. The unbeliever thinks he is wise in following natural reason, which leads him to think he can save himself. In their wisdom some unbelievers even conclude that there is nothing supernatural, in fact, that there is no God. But God calls atheists "fools" (Psalm 14:1). And "has not God made foolish the wisdom of the world?" (1 Corinthians 1:20). He has done so through "Christ the power of God and the wisdom of God" (1 Corinthians 1:24). To be without Christ is indeed to be "foolish."

When we were without Christ, Paul and Titus and we all were "disobedient, deceived and enslaved by all kinds of passions and pleasures." There is no need for a detailed description. Every day the press and the airwaves describe the wretchedness and folly of the world without Christ. With it all, there is the self-deception. People are deceived into thinking that disobedience is a right, that immorality is freedom, that their foolishness is wisdom.

As the world of unbelievers, of which we "at one time" were a part, pursues all kinds of passions and pleasures, this leads to lives filled with "malice and envy," to "being hated and hating one another." The bitter fruit that envy and hatred bear is abuse, crime and murder. We see it daily. What a miserable world this would be if God left it to itself! How miserable we would be if God had left us to ourselves! But God didn't!

God's Kindness and Love

4But when the kindness and love of God our Savior appeared, 5he saved us, not because of righteous things we had done, but because of his mercy. He saved us through the washing of rebirth and renewal by the Holy Spirit, 6whom he poured out on us generously through Jesus Christ our Savior, 7so that, having been justified by his grace, we might become heirs having the hope of eternal life.

This is one of the choicest passages of Holy Scripture. In one sentence in the original Greek, Paul sums up the entire gospel. What a change this proclaims after being reminded of what we "at one time" were!

The gospel Paul presents tells us that "He [God] saved us." It is a message of salvation. Paul also speaks of "having been justified." The gospel tells us we have been justified, that is, declared just, or righteous. God is "not counting men's sins against them." "God made him who had no sin to be sin for us, so that in him we might become the righteousness of God" (2 Corinthians 5:19,21).

It is significant that God, here referring to the Father, is called "our Savior." Also Jesus Christ, who is the Son of God, in this passage is called "our Savior." And the Holy Spirit is mentioned as being "poured out on us generously through Jesus Christ." The God of the gospel, the God who saves, is the one who is Father, Son and Holy Spirit, the only true God.

Why did God save us? What moved him? As always, Paul rules out anything on our part: "not because of righteous things we had done." How fortunate! Looking again at verse 3 we realize that we never could have done any "righteous things." If God were to wait with granting us salvation until he saw something righteous in us, we never would be saved.

What moved God? Four characteristics are attributed to God. First are "the kindness and love of God our Savior." "Kindness" speaks of the good will God has toward us, that he is disposed to bless us. The word for "love" used here is the same as our English word philanthropy, love of mankind. "God . . . loved the world," that is, the world of human beings, mankind. In Jesus the "kindness and love of God our Savior appeared." Look at Jesus and you see the Father's love and kindness actively present among us. "This is how God showed his love among us: He sent his one and only Son into the world that we might live through him" (1 John 4:9).

Two more words tell us why God saved us. He did so "because of his mercy." God looked with pity upon our wretchedness, with compassion that knew no limits. Our God is "rich in mercy" (Ephesians 2:4). God saved us also "by his grace." This is God's undeserved love. "For it is by grace you have been saved" (Ephesians 2:8). Nothing in us moved God to save, only his kindness, love, mercy and grace. That is the God revealed in the gospel. Look at him and be amazed!

How can I, a miserable sinner (remember verse 3), hope to receive this amazing gift of God? Jesus told Nicodemus, "No one can see the kingdom of God unless he is born again" (John 3:3). To Nicodemus, puzzled how one can be born again, Jesus explained: "No one can enter the kingdom of God unless he is born of water and the Spirit" (John 3:5). To Titus Paul writes: "He saved us through the washing of rebirth and renewal by the Holy Spirit." This is the "washing" that takes place in holy Baptism, a "washing" through which our sins are washed away (Acts 22:16), a "washing" that saves us (1 Peter 3:21). Paul writes to the Galatians: "For all of you who were baptized into Christ have clothed yourselves with Christ" (Galatians 3:27). By faith we now "wear," are covered with, the perfect righteousness and holiness that our Savior prepared for us through his life, death and resurrection. Baptism brings us into a faith-relationship with Christ. It brings about "rebirth," spiritual life. We celebrate our birthdays to remember when we came into this world with physical life. Even more important for us is the day of our baptism, our "rebirth" day.

Paul also calls it a washing of "renewal." The rebirth God effected in us by faith made of us "a new creation; the old has gone, the new has come!" (2 Corinthians 5:17). In writing to the Romans Paul describes what happens in Baptism: "We were therefore buried with him through baptism into death in order that, just as Christ was raised from the dead through the glory of the Father, we too may live a new life" (Romans 6:4). On the basis of this passage, Luther describes the meaning of baptism with these words: "It means that our Old Adam with his evil deeds and desires should be drowned by daily contrition and repentance, and die, and that day by day a new man should arise, as from the dead, to live in the presence of God in righteousness and purity now and forever." Truly baptism is a washing of regeneration and renewal.

All of this is the work of the Holy Spirit, whom God "poured out on us generously through Jesus Christ our Savior." When Jesus returned to the Father, he promised to send the Holy Spirit, the Counselor (John 15:26; 16:7; Acts 1:5). This he did on Pentecost day, and continues to do in baptism, in the Lord's Supper, indeed, whenever the gospel is preached.

Some people deny the saving power of baptism. Baptists and Pentecostals, for example, tell you that "you must be born again," that you must have a rebirth that the Holy Spirit brings about apart from baptism, in some direct manner that you can feel and experience in your heart. They separate the work of the Holy Spirit from baptism and the other means of grace. The fact remains, however, that Paul here speaks of a washing through which the Holy Spirit causes a rebirth and renewal. How this can be we do not understand. That this is what happens when we baptize with water in the name of the triune God we know and believe because God says so.

On the basis of these words in this letter to Titus, Luther gives the following answer to the question: "How can water do such great things?

"It is certainly not the water that does such things, but God's word which is in and with the water, and faith which trusts this word used with the water.

"For without God's word the water is just plain water and not Baptism. But with this word it is Baptism. God's word makes it a washing through which God graciously forgives our sins and grants us rebirth and a new life through the Holy Spirit."

The purpose of all this is "that, having been justified by his grace, we might become heirs having the hope of eternal life."

210

God has written us into his will as heirs. The inheritance is eternal life. That is our "hope" as God's heirs. It is a sure hope, for God will never change his will. So certain is this inheritance that Jesus speaks of eternal life as already ours: "Whoever believes in the Son has eternal life" (John 3:36). We have life now and will have it forever. What blessings we have in this life! What a glorious future awaits us in eternity!

8This is a trustworthy saying. And I want you to stress these things, so that those who have trusted in God may be careful to devote themselves to doing what is good. These things are excellent and profitable for everyone.

"This is a trustworthy saying." In the original, Paul emphasizes "trustworthy" by placing it at the beginning. The gospel as Paul has summed it up once more is indeed worthy of our trust, our faith, our full confidence. We can rely upon it totally. Paul wants Titus to stress "these things," this trustworthy message in all its completeness. The purpose is that "those who have trusted in God may be careful to devote themselves to doing what is good." Truly, the gospel can change hearts so that Christians will be moved to serve God in all they do. Paul shows Titus and every pastor that when we encourage Christians in their lives of sanctification, we must motivate them by "stressing" what God has done for them. Indeed, "these things are excellent and profitable for everyone." Let every pastor and teacher, let all Christians remember this!

Avoid Foolish Controversy and Divisive Persons

9But avoid foolish controversies and genealogies and arguments and quarrels about the law, because these are unprofitable and useless. 10Warn a divisive person once, and then warn him a second time. After that, have nothing to do with

211

him. [11]You may be sure that such a man is warped and sinful; he is self-condemned.

Paul had just instructed Titus to remind and encourage Christians to follow the things that are "excellent and profitable for everyone." Now as he concludes his letter he once more impresses on Titus to avoid what is "unprofitable and useless." Not only must we teach the truth faithfully, but pastors must also warn against what is foolish and false.

Paul refers to specific examples of useless teaching: "foolish controversies and genealogies and arguments and quarrels about the law." He referred to these in his letter to Timothy written about the same time (1 Timothy 1:3-7). In religious matters it is useless and unprofitable to speculate about things not revealed in Scripture. Some of these are of a less important nature. For example, Scripture does not tell us how old Mary was when she gave birth to Jesus. Whoever insists that she was sixteen years of age, and keeps on trying to convince others of this, is engaging in fruitless speculation. We are to avoid being drawn into such a controversy. People can become so engrossed in such foolish, useless controversy that they forget what is most important, that Mary's child is the holy Son of God, their Savior.

Other speculations and false teachings are of a more serious nature. For example, to deny the virgin birth is to deny a clearly revealed truth of Scripture and Jesus' divinity. Concerning such "deceivers" Paul instructs Titus: "Rebuke them sharply, so that they will be sound in the faith" (Titus 1:13).

Our curiosity wants to add to God's revelation. Our reason wants to speculate on matters we cannot understand, and change what God has made known. False teaching of every kind must be avoided.

How is Titus then to conduct himself toward those who are the false teachers? "Warn a divisive person once, and then warn him a second time." Not only are the teachings to be avoided, but the persons who teach falsely are, first, to be warned. Paul calls such a person "divisive." The Greek word used here gives us the word "heretic," and literally means "able to take or choose." The *God's Word to the Nations* translation includes this thought by translating: "a person who chooses to be different in his teaching." A false teacher, or heretic, has chosen to teach what is different from God's revealed truth. That makes him a divisive person. By teaching others what is contrary to Scripture he creates a division among the believers.

Paul tells Titus to warn such a person. He must be shown his error. If he is not convinced the first time, Titus is to warn him a second time. This is not a mechanical rule as though Titus must never warn anyone more often than twice. We are, however, not to just keep on warning. Rejected warnings must lead to further action. If the heretic continues to choose his own false teaching even after the "second" warning, "have nothing to do with him." No longer is Titus to consider him a brother in the faith. The false teacher by his false teaching causes division. By not having anything to do with him (not continuing in religious fellowship) we acknowledge the division he has caused.

To be united in a common faith in the Lord Jesus establishes a wonderful relationship among Christians. It is a distinct blessing to be able to go to the Lord together in prayer, to unite in singing his praises, to comfort one another with the promises we all hold dear, to share in bringing the saving gospel to a pagan world. Let us not fail to appreciate the blessing and joy of unity of faith on the basis of all that Scripture teaches. That is why we will regularly want to practice and enjoy Christian fellowship in divine worship with our congregation. That is why we gratefully participate in doing the Lord's work together with the many Christians with whom we share a common faith in our church body or synod.

False doctrine, however, disrupts this unity. The Lord Jesus warns us to be on our guard against false prophets (Matthew 7:15). Scripture clearly and repeatedly teaches us to avoid those who disrupt the fellowship by persisting in their false teachings and sinful life (Romans 16:17; Galatians 1:8,9; 2 John 9-11). Even when this involves excommunication, the purpose is always to regain the sinner whose course is leading to eternal damnation (Matthew 18:15ff; 1 Corinthians 5:1-5). What is more, such separation can prevent the error from infecting the entire body with its destructive poison (Romans 16:18; 1 Corinthians 5:6; Galatians 5:9; 2 Timothy 2:16,17).

Paul concludes this point by describing the divisive person: "You may be sure that such a man is warped and sinful; he is self-condemned." By not letting himself be corrected through the clear teaching of Scripture, he shows he is not thinking straight. He may not consciously be aware of this and may have blinded his reason and dulled his conscience. Nevertheless, by continuing in his false teaching he is sinning. He has condemned himself by his persistent rejection of the truth. "The heretic has condemned himself by the very fact that he by his own deliberate choice rejects the truth which has been shown to him. This does not necessarily mean that he acknowledges or recognizes that he is an errorist. He may very well have **deceived himself**. . . . But the fact that he rejects the truth in spite of the fact that it has been pointed out to him a number of times condemns him" (Gawrisch).

In his pastoral letters Paul repeatedly shows his concern about false teachings and false teachers. A church that is not serious in upholding the truth of the gospel will not long have it to proclaim. Paul, who has no equal in his zeal for missions, also has no equal in his zeal for the truth.

CONCLUDING INSTRUCTIONS
AND GREETING
TITUS 3:12-15

[12]As soon as I send Artemas or Tychicus to you, do your best to come to me at Nicopolis, because I have decided to winter there. [13]Do everything you can to help Zenas the lawyer and Apollos on their way and see that they have everything they need. [14]Our people must learn to devote themselves to doing what is good, in order that they may provide for daily necessities and not live unproductive lives.

Several final remarks conclude the letter. Paul had left Titus in Crete to "straighten out what was left unfinished" (1:5). This was a temporary assignment. He wanted Titus to rejoin him in Nicopolis, where he expected to spend the winter. The congregations in Crete were not to be without the leadership they still needed. Paul promises to send one of his trusted associates to replace Titus. This is the only reference to Artemas in the New Testament. References to Tychicus occur in Acts 20:4; Ephesians 6:21,22; Colossians 4:7; and 2 Timothy 4:12. These show Paul's frequent use of Tychicus as an emissary.

We do not know where Paul intended to go from Nicopolis (very likely the one located on the west coast of Greece). Winter would not be a good time for further travel, especially if it were by sea. We can assume that Paul had work in this region with which he wanted Titus to help him. Besides, it would be a time for these church leaders and friends to consult with one another, plan together and encourage one another for further mission work. Congregations should remember that the time their pastors and teachers spend at conferences and meetings with their fellow workers can serve to encourage, inspire and strengthen the church's leaders for their difficult tasks.

Zenas and Apollos are two further associates of Paul who, it is believed, were sent by him to bring this letter to Titus. Zenas is called a lawyer, whether in Jewish or Roman law we do not know. Apollos is also mentioned in Acts 18:24-28; 19:1; 1 Corinthians 1:12; 16:12. Paul does not say where these two men were going from Crete, but he asks Titus to help them on their way. We may conclude that they were on a mission journey, and in this way their needs were to be provided.

Titus was not to be alone in providing for these men. "Our people must learn to devote themselves to doing what is good, in order that they may provide for daily necessities and not live unproductive lives." In this context "doing what is good" surely included working faithfully at their place of employment. "Provide for daily necessities" included the necessities of Zenas and Apollos as they continued on their way. Thus their lives would be productive and fruitful. What we give toward the support of training and sending out missionaries, and that is the basic work of a church body, makes also our lives fruitful as servants of God and as members of the fellowship of believers. Pastors are to encourage their members to be fruitful also in this way.

15Everyone with me sends you greetings. Greet those who love us in the faith.

Grace be with you all.

217

The letter ends with greetings. Titus knew where Paul was writing from and who was with Paul. So he knew who was included in "everyone," even though this information eludes us.

Paul's greetings are extended to "those who love us in the faith." Truly, faith in the Lord Jesus establishes a special bond of love among Christians. Paul expresses that by his greeting, even though he does not mention any of them by name. "Grace be with you all." This closing wish is meant for all to whom Paul extends greetings, for all who read this letter. Both in the opening and closing greeting, as in all of his letters, Paul speaks of grace. His mission was to proclaim the riches of God's grace in Christ. He had nothing better to wish anyone in greeting them. Neither do we. Grace be with you all!

* * * * * * * * *

Pastoral letters — what an inspiration they must have been to pastors Timothy and Titus! How effectively the Holy Spirit must have worked in the hearts of the original readers of these inspired words from God's chosen missionary! May the Holy Spirit similarly use these letters to instruct, encourage and inspire those who are called to serve God's people in every generation. May they help God's people to appreciate those the Lord sends, to rejoice in his saving gospel, and to live the gospel by the Spirit's power.